# Music with the Brain in Mind

Eric Jensen

**CORWIN PRESS**
A SAGE Publications Company
Thousand Oaks, California

*For information:*

Corwin Press
A Sage Publications Company
2455 Teller Road
Thousand Oaks, California 91320
www.corwinpress.com

Sage Publications Ltd.
1 Oliver's Yard
55 City Road
London EC1Y 1SP
United Kingdom

Sage Publications India Pvt. Ltd.
B-42 Panchsheel Enclave
Post Box 4109
New Delhi 110 017  India

Printed in the United States of America.

The author would like to acknowledge the following individuals: Dr. Lawrence Parsons, Dr. Gordon Shaw, and Dr. Norman Weinberger; special thanks to the MUSICA newsletter; to the countless music advocates who are making a difference everyday; to Don Campbell who planted the seeds in me to write this book; to Bob Sylwester who inspired me to think about the topic in a novel way; to jazz pianist Harry Pickens, whose music has brought joy to my soul; and to my researcher extraordinaire Rick Crowley.

Note:
In the writing of *Music with the Brain in Mind*, no financial support or any other form of endorsement was received from organizations or individuals that could possibly be construed as representing conflict of interest or a biased perspective for commercial gain.

ISBN #1-890460-06-0

This book is printed on acid-free paper.

06  07  08  09  10  9  8  7  6  5  4  3  2

Music is a language
that kindles the human spirit,
sharpens the mind,
fuels the body,
and fills the heart.

# Contents

# Preface

**C**ompelling evidence supports the position that, when implemented properly, the musical arts can provide a positive, significant, and lasting benefit to learners. The supporting research is significant, due in part to its diversity and depth. If this were a court of law, the ruling would be clear: Music in education is valuable "beyond a reasonable doubt."

Our desire to express ourselves through the musical arts is innate, and its purpose may extend far beyond mere pleasure. Some believe, in fact, that our neurobiological system is virtually dependent upon music for its complete development. As such, the biological value of music likely exceeds the evidence that listening to it can boost jigsaw puzzle skills as some research suggests. Neurobiologist Mark Jude Tramo of Harvard Medical School says, "Music is biologically part of human life, just as it is aesthetically part of human life."

In discussing the benefits of music, we've ascribed them to two general categories: (1) benefits as a *direct* result of music; and (2) benefits as an *indirect* result of music. Also, for the purpose of this book, the terms "music" and "the musical arts" are used interchangeably and are meant to encompass the whole gamut of music playing and listening elements. Although singing in the shower, playing the guitar, or acting in a musical performance falls within the framework, so does composing, reading, analyzing, arranging, and creating music of any kind.

If strong evidence supports the value of music in education, why are we still fighting for its inclusion in our schools? This is a complex question with a variety of answers. First, many educators don't know enough about the brain and learning to be able to articulate the value of music to policy-influencing bodies. Second, most teachers don't have a music background, nor do traditional teacher preparation programs train us to incorporate music into the curriculum. Third, all educators are constrained by competing demands on their time and resources, curriculum mandates, and various bureaucratic restraints. And fourth, the policy-making boards that are making curriculum decisions are primarily interested in the input-output ratio—that is, cost per student per year in relation to test scores. But, as you'll soon discover, the musical arts are not about school efficiency in the old-style sense. Rather, incorporating music into the standard curriculum is about effectiveness, and nourishing learners and their brain for the long haul—a concept that, in the end, may simply develop better citizens for tomorrow.

# PART ONE:

# Building a Music Foundation

- ◆ How Do We Value Music?

- ◆ Can Music Pass the Test?

- ◆ How Do We Hear Music?

- ◆ Where in the Brain is Music?

# How Do We Value Music?

*T*his book is about the value of the musical arts in educating our students. Its primary purpose is to broaden the discourse and strengthen the position of music's positive effects on the brain. It offers not only plausible theories that may help explain how music optimizes learning, but it supports these theories with solid research studies—both quantitative and qualitative. It also provides practical strategies for incorporating music into the curriculum.

With the well-meaning, but short-sighted, thrust "back to basics" over the past decade, many schools across the country have relegated their music offerings to extracurricular activities, or worse, withdrawn them altogether. In response, many educators, parents, and students have questioned this decision, and hence, more attention than ever has been cast upon music's role and its value in the curriculum.

While some music program supporters have shied away from claiming a scientific basis to support their argument for music, I disagree. Clearly the scientific evidence is only one way to support the importance of music in our schools, but in a world that places great emphasis on the rational/experimental model of inquiry, ignoring this line of reasoning doesn't make sense.

While there are some studies that support the cognitive benefits of a musical arts curriculum, critics have noted that not all of them are peer-reviewed, longitudinal, statistically significant, or well designed (Eisner 1998). Indeed, research designs, whether qualitative or quantitative, can be faulty, and in this author's opinion, many more well-designed studies are needed. In spite of this, a strong case for music inclusion, as you will see in the second part of this book, can be made. But first, let's explore some of the formidable challenges facing school music programs today.

# THE CHALLENGES

Although the physiological benefits of the musical arts are sprinkled across the neural spectrum—from more fine motor control and released creativity to better emotional regulation—the intricacy of the brain means that results can take *time* and may not immediately boost test scores. Yet, the dominant educational paradigm tends to value that which is expediently measured. If higher tests scores are what is valued (and if the tests measure only math, problem-solving, and verbal skills), the musical arts are at a clear disadvantage. In a society that finds delayed gratification an undesirable notion and quick results the ideal, again the musical arts are at a clear disadvantage. The reason is obvious: The arts are inefficient—results are not necessarily immediate, nor are they always measurable.

Much of the contribution that music makes to the minds and hearts of our students, takes months or years to show up. It will be evidenced, but often after the policy-makers who influenced the curriculum decisions in the first place have moved on to their next political pastime. They've missed the beat, and once again our students are cheated out of developing their musical minds.

Another problem with music inclusion is that most teachers don't have a music background, nor are they taught in teacher education programs how to incorporate music into the curriculum. In addition, how many of us have time to carry out a multi-year crusade directed at school boards and national decision makers in an effort to get music programs (or any program for that matter) recognized and accepted? When most policy makers and politicians are only interested in the input-output ratio—that is, cost per student per year in relation to immediate test scores—the scenario is disheartening. Even students may narrow their focus to achieve better grades in the areas deemed "important" by the institution. The old factory model of education that puts cost effectiveness and *measurable* results above *authentic* learning poses a great challenge to educators who believe in the efficacy of music. Although teachers (and students) may recognize music's importance, they are stymied by its lack of support at the leadership level.

In an effort to justify music programs, some researchers have taken an approach that asks questions like, Does music help math? Might it help language development? Can it be applied to science? These inquiries are fair game. But the bigger question is, Why is there a need to validate music in standard curriculum terms? We don't, for example, ask if math or science learning helps develop music skills, do we? And ultimately, even when music is shown quantitatively to aid in the learning of other disciplines, the next argument is, But how efficient is the process?

If students learn about history through the musical arts, couldn't they learn it faster with a more direct approach? If a marching band practices for one hundred minutes a day for one hundred days to perform in a ninety-minute parade, is this good use of time? And what about the student who invests years to learn an instrument with only marginal artistic results? So, if the musical arts are inefficient, why include them? Because the musical arts promote the development of necessary and valuable human neurobiological functions, in spite of the fact that such learning may go undetected by standardized tests. Today we have the knowledge to articulate the brain's functional responses to music in ways that are supported by the research. Granted, other more widely accepted disciplines have not had to justify their existence, but maybe they should.

## THE BENEFITS

The evidence suggests that musical arts are central to learning. The systems they nourish (which include our integrated sensory, attentional, cognitive, emotional, and motor capacity processes) are in fact, the driving force behind all other learning. This doesn't mean that one *can't* learn without the arts; many have. But learning with the arts provides more opportunity to develop these multiple brain systems, none of which is easy to quantify due to the nature of the process.

Processes are essential in that they mediate later results, but testing a process is, at best, problematic. To use a simple analogy, consider that a cake's ingredients might be perfectly measured and blended, but when removed from the oven too soon or evaluated too frequently, the darn thing falls. On the other hand, the cake might look great, but taste bad. When it comes to the brain and learning, there are many variables that can't be controlled. On the other hand, with the advent of sophisticated neuroimaging devices, scientists are making huge strides in the study of cognitive processes. We now have the capability to see what is happening in the brain as subjects listen to, analyze, or play music.

And finally, another consideration is that, while the cognitive benefits of music are significant, the non-academic benefits are also vastly under-recognized. If music is widely known to support relaxation, creativity, self-discipline, and motivation, why aren't we touting this from the highest rungs of the academic ladder? Who hasn't experienced the impact of music on these areas of their life? Beyond that, consider how music has impacted your own aesthetic awareness, cultural exposure, social harmony, emotional expression, appreciation of diversity, and sense of self—the virtual underpinnings of a healthy culture! The musical arts should be valued in schools not only because the emerging science supports them, but because the dynamic and broad-based appeal of music is equivalent to other widely accepted disciplines.

# Can Music Pass the Test?

Like mathematics, music is a universal language with a symbolic way of representing the world. And, like mathematics, the musical arts allow us to communicate with others, while illuminating and recording human insights. But music contributes to a slew of other human needs, as well. It extends our understanding of other people and provides for healthy emotional expression. Music lifts our spirits and brings joy to our soul. It impacts academic achievement, perceptual-motor skills, and social skills. And, it provides for the essential qualities that represent culture—imagination, community, energy, and creativity; qualities we need most as we enter this new century.

Your native tongue is a language; mathematics is a language; and to an extent, emotions are a language. The thesis here is that music really deserves a place among the ranks of these critical subjects as important representations of our world. The common misconception that music is a fringe activity—that it is less than a "major discipline"—represents a societal ignorance of sorts. This chapter explores the arguments for reconsidering the musical arts among the major disciplines.

The seven criteria I've identified as useful in determining what is critical to the curriculum are outlined below. The major disciplines, like science or languages, you'll find hold up well against these criteria, but what happens when we examine the musical arts from this perspective? Let's take a look.

## 1. Is the subject assessable?

While it's relatively difficult to assess the musical arts, it can and has been done. For example, in Wisconsin a coalition of arts educators has developed a comprehensive quality arts assessment program that has been recognized by state leaders. There is much value in creating strong assessment procedures that recognize the characteristics and limitations inherent in teaching and learning the musical arts. Other organizations and school districts have also done an admirable job of developing measurable criteria for evaluating the musical arts.

*Grade for the musical arts: passing!*

# 2. Is it brain-based?

Are structures or mechanisms for music actually built into the brain? Are there identifiable areas of the brain that respond to learning? In the late 1970s and early 80s, a myth pervaded the academic community that the arts were just a right-brained frill. This hang-over from the "left brain is logical; right brain is creative" line of thinking, which was faulty in itself, has wreaked havoc ever since. It turns out that the musical arts not only engage many areas of the brain, but also have multiple and far-reaching effects on the mind. Yes, we can say that music has a biological basis.

*Grade for the musical arts: passing!*

# 3. Is it culturally necessary?

A discipline should serve clear cultural needs. It ought to promote the betterment of humanity, or at least the local culture. It's an easy argument to make: Learn science; invent a vaccine (like Jonas Salk did for polio); and you've done a lot of good. But in what ways might the musical arts serve humanity? Here the answer is clear. They promote social skills that enhance awareness of others and tolerance for differences. They promote unity and harmony. They enhance cognitive and perceptual skills. They serve as vehicles for cultural identity and free expression.

*Grade for the musical arts: passing!*

# 4. What are the downside risks?

The downside scenario of learning a discipline must be minimal, if not nonexistent. The critical questions here are, Could the subject impede the learning of other disciplines? Or, Could the subject harm an individual or group of learners in any other way? For example, there are no known cases in which an arts curriculum, either integrated or modular, has been faulted for *lowering* student test scores, increasing behavior problems, or reducing graduation rates. However, even when arts teaching is provided in a substandard manner (i.e., at the exclusion of other subjects), benefits are still derived by the learner.

*Grade for the musical arts: passing!*

# 5. Is it inclusive?

To be a major discipline, it cannot be elitist. In other words, it must be something that can be learned, if not mastered, by the overwhelming majority of learners. Since we know that all levels of society create and respond to the musical arts, this criteria is well-served by music. Music, in fact, breaks down barriers between races, religions, cultures, geographic distinctions, and socioeconomic strata. The Suzuki Method exemplifies that with the proper instruction, most everyone can learn to play music. The musical arts have the capacity to engage us all.
*Grade for the musical arts: passing!*

# 6. Is there survival value in it?

Survival of the species is still a critical consideration as an approach to education. Just as there is clear survival benefits to learning how to speak, read, write, inquire, and compute, a community's survival is based not only on the cognitive strengths of its members, but on the unity and tenacity of the culture, as well. The musical arts help to define and support and transmit this culture from one generation to the next. The detailed work of cultural anthropologists Kathryn Coe (1990) and Ellen Dissayanake (1988) have helped demonstrate that art-making has been present throughout civilization, that it is a necessary part of life, that it transmits important societal values, and that it facilitates the creation of strong and large communities.
*Grade for the musical arts: passing!*

# 7. Is it wide-ranging?

The discipline must have subdisciplines that bring breadth, depth, and credibility to the major discipline. We all know how broad and deep the discipline of science is niched out—from biology, astronomy, and chemistry to geology, physics, and electronics. An entire sub-world thrives within the "box" called science. But the musical arts can hold its head just as high. Among its ranks is performance music, music listening, song writing, arranging, analysis, singing, improvisation, and conducting. Taken as a whole, the musical arts are wide ranging and deep in substance.
*Grade for the musical arts: passing!*

While the musical arts should not be held to any *more* of a rigorous scrutiny than the other major disciplines, it should also not be held to any *less* of a standard. Once educators can see how music learning compares to the traditional curriculum, the most important next step is to recognize that music belongs in the standard curriculum, not when there's an available teacher by chance, or the physical education class is rained out, or there's a substitute teacher for the day, or a student is labeled "gifted," or "learning disabled," or "emotionally disturbed," but every day, at every grade level, and in every school. No ifs, ands, or buts about it, music needs to be integrated into the standard curriculum.

By itself, music will not save schools that are struggling, but it will indeed play a positive part. We all know that it's not the *quantity* of assignments that makes a student smart: It's *how* students learn to *think about* the material. Learners need to address difficult questions and challenging projects with time to ponder, reflect, and inquire. The more disciplines involved, the better. The more encompassing the topic, the better. The less trivial and the more in-depth analysis about the things that matter most in our world—order, integrity, critical-thinking skills, a sense of wonder, truth, flexibility, fairness, dignity, personal responsibility, justice, creative expression, and cooperation—the better. Does this sound like a tall order? It may be, but these values have been passed down through generations for centuries, in large part by valuing artistic expression. We need more music in the curriculum because to ignore the musical arts is to disregard our cultural heritage and to distance students from their musical birthright.

# THE WALDORF MODEL

Perhaps one of the best long-term models for examining the process and results of integrating music into the curriculum is the Waldorf School. For more than 50 years, learners attending Waldorf education programs have had the opportunity to explore their musical interests through standard curriculum activities. As an independent, arts-centered learning institution, the Waldorf School is one of the fastest-growing education enterprises in the world: Today there are 130 Waldorf schools in America and 700 worldwide.

In Waldorf schools, students often spend a year working on a single project like building a piece of furniture or learning to play a musical instrument. Community service projects, exposure to the arts, and music interactions are considered good use of valuable class time. This kind of seemingly "loosey-goosey" schooling can really test the patience of some anxious parents.

For straight-line, conservative, standards-seeking, bean-counting, highly competitive parents, the Waldorf philosophy may, in fact, seem outrageous. The teachers avoid textbooks, heap on field trips, encourage journal reflections, and downplay tests. A practice called "looping" keeps teachers with their students for years—usually from first through eighth grade—while placing great value on long-term relationships. Waldorf schools never force reading on students; they focus instead on the love and joy languages and literature can provide. Often Waldorf children don't start to read until they're seven to nine years old, and, understandably, some parents panic and pull their children out.

But something must be working. Prominent educational figures including Howard Gardner and Theodore Sizer express admiration for this method. On SAT exams, Waldorf students exceed national averages. They often pass achievement tests at double or triple the rate for public school students (Oppenheimer 1999). College professors remark about the humility, sense of wonder, concentration, and intellectual resourcefulness of Waldorf graduates. These lean-budgeted, small private schools have produced the likes of Oscar-winning actor Paul Newman, Nobel novelist Saul Bellow, and legendary dancer Mikhail Baryshnikov. The Waldorf curriculum, which is heavily grounded in the arts and particularly music, exposes all first graders to their own (likely first) musical instrument—a recorder. Their instrument is stored in a case they build themselves. Beyond this, the school offers jazz, choir, orchestra, and more. A day may start with singing and end with a dramatic performance. All this is offered along with the subjects of science, history, literature, and math, but they learn these through the process of the arts. Naturally, there are thousands of other examples of schools worldwide that also emphasize music and are successful, but it doesn't take a private school to make it happen. Any school can do it.

# How Do We Hear Music?

Our system of hearing, which most of us take for granted, is really a highly complex series of steps that begins with the flaps of flesh we commonly call ears. These outer "auricles," however, are merely nature's way of funneling sounds to our brain. Sounds out beyond our bodies begin as pressure waves which vibrate toward us. The pressure expeditiously moves through our external auditory canal and bangs into our ear drum, where the acoustic energy is transformed into mechanical energy. When sound rattles the ear drum, which is connected to small vibrating bones called ossicles, this sensitive hardware acts as both an amplifier and volume surge protector. It focuses and builds up sounds when necessary and dampens them when the decibels are too high.

The most impressive action takes place in the middle or inner ear where the ossicles transmit the sounds to our internal concert hall. The inner ear houses the cochlea, a fluid-lined coil the shape of a curled up snail and covered with specialized neurons called hair cells. As the vibrations from noise or music ripple through the fluid, they prod different hair neurons that are tuned to different sound frequencies. A paltry 14,000 receptor cells are oscillating and signaling the 32,000 nerve fibers (axons) that leave this area headed towards your brain.

*The Auditory Pathways*

Think for a moment of an oversold rock concert or an intensely crowded, high velocity, body-slamming, teen dance club. Imagine that each participant is a molecule shaking and bouncing from 20 to 20,000 times per second. Next, multiply this event by millions; then imagine trying to interpret a collective message that includes input from every one of these wildly oscillating dancers. As these sounds reach the cochlea, they're converted into nerve impulses. This is what your inner ear does every day, all day. Each fibre of the cochlear nerve is selectively tuned to a characteristic frequency determined by its location. Once the sound waves have connected with hair neurons that match their frequency, the cochlea's job is done. The frequency activates the neurons and the mechanical energy is now turned into electrical energy. The first place in the brain these neurons project to is the brainstem in the cochlear nucleus of the medulla. This area receives projections from contralateral ears, and it helps us determine the location of sounds. In the brain, communication is a two way street. At this juncture, there are also projections from the auditory cortex that send information back to the cochlea to aid in both learned and novel auditory discrimination.

*The Inner Ear*

**Cupula displacement causes movement of the cilia on hair cells that are embedded within this substance.**

**Angular Acceleration**

**Endolymph Flow**

**Ampullar Nerve**

**Ampillary crest contains hair cells, and stretching from it to the roof is the cupula–a gelatinous material.**

Next the electrical package called music is sent to the thalamus for a quick stop at the medial geniculate nucleus. Subsequently, these impulses flow to the auditory cortex on the left side of the brain. This area projects to the superior temporal gyrus, known as Broadman's area 41 and 42, your auditory cortex. These are the areas that "light up" the most during PET or fMRI scans when sounds are presented.

Now, to put it all together, your brain has developed elaborate neural networks called feature detectors. These are able to process specific components of music like pitch, timbre, harmony, and rhythm. These networks develop in response to the kind of music you listen to—meaning what you listen to changes how your brain is configured (Furman 1978).

The process by which music gets processed is even more complex. In a moment, known as the perceptual present, we can sense, sort, categorize, recognize, and respond to music. This rate of time (we'll call it "response time") is governed by the speed at which neurons can fire, connect, and oscillate. Estimates of response time vary depending on the listener's experience, but the consensus is that it is generally in the neighborhood of two seconds. We actually grasp a piece of music in bits and bites, and anticipate by filling in what we cannot process.

*Key Areas of Musical Processing (Part 1)*

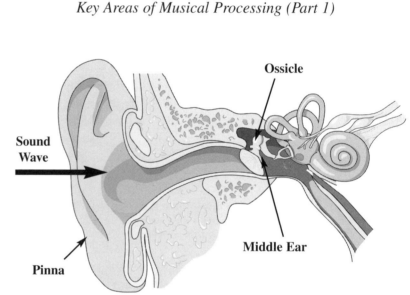

Consequently, only part of a three-minute composition is fully absorbed, but we may feel as if we've absorbed it all. What's most essential here is that our brain plays an active part in the hearing process: It is by no means a passive participant.

The harmonic structure, interval, quality, timbre, and the spatial, temporal, and long-term patterns of music are recognized by our brain's nondominant hemisphere (in most of us, this is the right hemisphere). The short-term signatures, like rapid variance in volume, rapid and accurate pitch trajectory, pacing, and lyrics, are recognized by our brain's dominant hemisphere (in most of us, this is the left hemisphere). However, all this happens too fast for conscious awareness.

In listening to longer compositions, like a symphony, our brain is likely absorbing less than one percent of the musical data, yet we aren't aware of this. We detect pitch after just one hundredth of a second, loudness in a twentieth of a second, and timbre at a tenth of a second. For comparison, we detect consonants in about a tenth of a second (Jourdain 1997). To close with the analogy we started with, the brain experiences sounds like a huge slam-dancing concert, yet somehow we are able to identify, group, and synthesize the pieces, in a way that brings form to the sensations. This experience is what we call music.

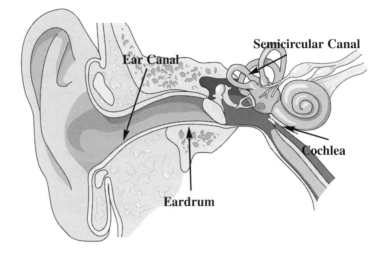

*Key Response Areas of Musical Processing (Part 2)*

# Where in the Brain is Music?

Most of us are the "practical sort," wanting to know exactly of what use something is before investing time in learning it. Given this, does it really matter where in the brain musical activations occur? The answer is yes and here's why. If specific musical activations share the same precise locations, for example, as mathematical activities, then the hypothesis that there is a positive relationship between music and math is strengthened. But the fact is, music activates most places in the brain depending on the type of experimental model used and the subject tested.

When subjects are asked to identify the individual elements inherent in music, the brain selectively activates various areas to isolate and detect them. The area of the brain that processes, for example, *where* the music is coming from is different from the area that processes *what kind* of music it is. Many studies have compared the brain activation patterns of musicians versus subjects with no musical background. In one study, subjects listened to approximately one hundred selections, consisting of familiar music, novel music, then notes with timbre, pitch, and rhythm changes, while PET scans measured the areas of brain activation. The following findings were obtained:

◆ Familiar music selections activated Broca's area (located in the left hemisphere), suggesting that all familiar sounds, not just word sounds, may get processed in this area. The exception was when the listener was trying to remember a musical title.

◆ Rhythm notes also activated Broca's area and the cerebellum.

◆ Harmony activated the left side of the brain more than right, as well as the inferior temporal cortex.

◆ Timbre activated the right hemisphere. This was the only musical element that did.

◆ Pitch activated an area on the left back of the brain called the precuneus. Another area involved may be the right auditory cortex.

◆ Melody activated both sides of the brain.

These findings remind us that music is *not* exclusively a "right-brained" activity, a common fallacy. It's interesting to note that brain activation in nonmusician subjects when listening to either words (consonant-vowel combinations) or music as an instrument was played, follows predictable responses. While background music activates the right hemisphere to a greater degree, concentration on the lyrics activates the left hemisphere. And correspondingly, a right-ear superiority in performance of words and a left-ear superiority in performance of music was noted. This reminds us that words with music activates the brain differently than purely instrumental music.

While there is certainly substantial activation in the temporal lobes, there is also activation in the left inferior frontal lobe, right dorsolateral prefrontal cortex, left occipital lobe, and the cerebellum in response to music (Bronnick, et al. 1999). These lesser activations are important to keep in mind when making statements about what areas of the brain music activates. Some research has noted even greater brain-area activation during sight-reading and music playing (Sergent, et al. 1992). Performance demands may require processing by every lobe and the cerebellum.

While patients with lesions or other forms of brain damage can provide valuable information about the localization of music-related attentional systems, imaging tools are also useful. One PET scan study that examined activation patterns during particular task performances revealed a task-dependent hemispheric bias. In the study, which asked subjects to compare the pitch of the first two melodies with the pitch of the last two, the right hemisphere showed greater activation (Zatorre, et al. 1994). This finding was later confirmed with a lesioning study.

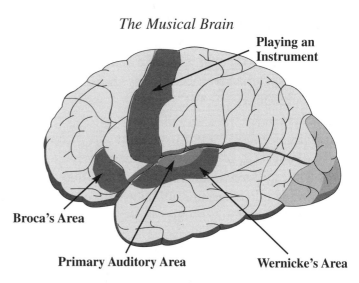

*The Musical Brain*

Playing an Instrument

Broca's Area

Primary Auditory Area

Wernicke's Area

If a particular area of the brain is specifically responsible for processing a particular musical element, then it would follow that damage to that area would impair this process. One study (Zatorre and Samson 1991) confirmed this hypothesis: Right-hemisphere damage impairs the ability to process timbre in music. This result occurred in both musician and nonmusician subjects. We can also isolate the process of musical timing to the auditory cortex and rhythm to the left hemisphere, conceivably because processing rhythm requires attention to sequence and beat (Peretz and Morais 1993). Melody perception activates both hemispheres, but specific melody recognition mainly activates the right hemisphere (Matteis, et al. 1997). It's important to note here that listening to or for specific elements of music will produce a different activation pattern than simply listening to music for enjoyment.

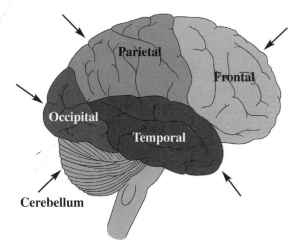

*Multiple Sites/Lobes Activated by Music*

Parietal

Frontal

Occipital

Temporal

Cerebellum

## DIFFERENTIATED BLOOD FLOW

Why do researchers care about blood flow? Because it tells us how active the brain is and where in the brain the activation is taking place. This information is useful for drawing parallels with cognition and creativity, which also have their own localized effects. Here's an example: When no music was presented, cerebral blood flow was very similar between autistic and nonautistic (control group) subjects (Garreau 1994). But when a tone was presented, the nonautistic group showed an increase in blood flow activation to the left temporal-occipital region and a generalized increase overall. Among autistics, however, whose blood flow diverges from the norm, the right temporal-occipital region was activated. This study suggests that there may be some linkage to laterality in blood flow and healthy responses. The researchers conducted two other studies that revealed the same results (ibid).

Interestingly enough, brain responses are different between nonmusicians and musicians exposed to music. Pioneering brain imager John Mazziotta measured blood flow and brain activity through brain scans while different learners listened to music. The novice's right hemisphere lit up when music was played while the musician's left hemisphere was more active when exposed to the same music. The musician also showed more activity in the limbic system. Mazziotti believes naive listeners have more right hemisphere activation, but experts have more left hemisphere activation.

The most plausible explanation is that "naive" listeners depend on melody for discrimination and pleasure while experts generally process music's more "language-like" sequences. If, however, musicians are processing highly complex music and listening for melodic contour, they'll activate the right hemisphere just as a nonmusician would (Vollmer-Haase, et al. 1998). This is congruent with evidence that shows an increase in blood flow in the right temporal lobe in response to melody listening (Bower 1994).

With the advent of brain-imaging devices, we learned that music activates many places in the brain. We can also now see how music impacts blood flow. While alone this finding may not seem earth-shaking, it lays the foundation for the subsequent thesis that music making impacts memory, stress, and the immune system, all of which are dependent on blood flow. Taken as a whole, these studies suggest that the various components of music are (1) able to be isolated; (2) able to be detected; and (3) dependent on the listener.

# SUMMARY OF BLOOD FLOW ACTIVATIONS

| Musical Element | Brain Area(s) Activated | Music Background |
|---|---|---|
| Composite Listening | L-Hemisphere/Auditory Cortex | Musician |
| Composite Listening | R-Hemisphere/Auditory Cortex | Non-Musician |
| Pitch | L-Hemisphere/Precuneus | Musician |
| Timbre | R-Hemisphere | Both Musicians and Non-Musicians |
| Melody | R-Temporal Lobe | Both |
| Rhythm | Broca's Area/Cerebellum | Both |
| Familiar Music | Broca's Area/L-Side | Both |
| Recalling a Song Title | L-Hemisphere/Temporal Lobe | Both |
| Understanding Lyrics | Wernicke's Area | Both |
| Playing Familiar Music | Cerebellum/Temporal/Parietal Lobes | Both |
| Playing Unfamiliar Music | Cerebellum/Temporal/Parietal/Frontal | Musician |
| Melodic Contour | R-Hemisphere/Auditory Cortex | Both |

# Part Two:

# Making a Case for Music

# The Biological Value of Music

Indeed it is a strong claim that music is a fundamental, essential human need, but when you consider the following, you see that the claim is substantial:

- Music provides adaptive value. Although the evidence is somewhat speculative, music probably enhances survival and is evidenced universally in all human cultures.

- Music's impact on the brain can be traced with neuroimaging tools such as ƒMRIs and PET scans. The actual brain pathways and mechanisms involved can be isolated. This suggests that the effects also happen on a physical level.

- The general consensus among researchers is that music commonly improves quality of life.

- Cortical lesions to particular brain areas impair musical talent. This demonstrates the specific built-in physicality of music-making structures.

- Extremes of musical talent have been evident throughout the ages. This suggests the plausibility of a genetic component.

These facts tell us a lot about the biological nature of music in our lives, but there's more. Music impacts the brain and body in many other ways—some temporary, lasting only minutes, and others more permanent. The arousal effect in *listening* is an example of the temporary, but powerful, impact music has on us, while brain changes as a result of long-term keyboard *playing* provide an example of music's more permanent influence. The neurobiological value of music is derived when the system is activated repeatedly over time. Naturally, the activation must be positive; that is, it must strengthen the organism's behavior in some way. The duration of the strengthening will vary depending on repetition and other variables. As such questions arise, what brain systems might be enhanced by a comprehensive musical arts program? And what evidence supports the hypothesis?

**The following five crucial neurobiological systems, and their respective subsets, each influence learning:**

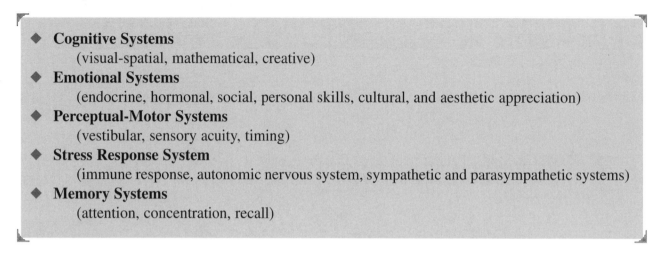

- ◆ **Cognitive Systems**
  (visual-spatial, mathematical, creative)
- ◆ **Emotional Systems**
  (endocrine, hormonal, social, personal skills, cultural, and aesthetic appreciation)
- ◆ **Perceptual-Motor Systems**
  (vestibular, sensory acuity, timing)
- ◆ **Stress Response System**
  (immune response, autonomic nervous system, sympathetic and parasympathetic systems)
- ◆ **Memory Systems**
  (attention, concentration, recall)

*Systems Impacted by Music Making*

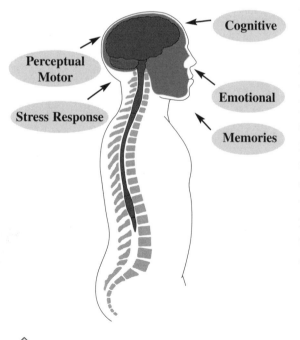

There is no other academic discipline that can be held to this stringent biological standard. In addition, the limitations of technology prevent us from making intrusive studies on our subjects. Having said that, we may, however, be able to build a circumstantial case. If music making contributes to the development of essential systems, there ought to be a plausible argument for how this happens, as well as supporting studies on the real-world effects. While we can identify a system (i.e., emotional), it's critical to understand that the human being is truly a system of systems. The emotional system impacts the cognitive system, which impacts the motor system, which impacts the immune system, and so on. There is no single system in the human body. Mind, body, emotions, immunity, and genes all play a role in the success of other systems.

The argument to support the claim that music plays an important biological role in our lives, is presented in the following pages. It's important to understand, however, that the word "proof" will not, and should not be used lightly when it comes to any scientific discussion. Again, it is hoped that these arguments will widen the public discourse and provide greater support for the value of the musical arts in education. First, we'll explore how your brain makes music out of noise; then, as promised, I offer seven reasons to support a strong arts program.

# Brains Built for Music

If the musical arts are essential to the development of important neurobiological systems, then we must ask ourselves, is this capacity innate? It's easy to argue that music entertains and soothes humans throughout their life, but the question is, "Is the need for music hard-wired into our biology?" This is a difficult and controversial question to answer because it requires some speculation from biology, ethnology, and anthropology. Noted cognitive scientist Steven Pinker says, "As far as biological cause and effect are concerned, music is useless" (Pinker 1997). However, he is in the minority.

If Darwin was right, traits and behaviors that enhance the survival of a species will be selected by nature because they better ensure the perpetuation of a species from one generation to the next. Could the use of music increase survival chances? Recently, some researchers, including Dr. Bjorn Mekur studied this question (Wallin, et al. 1999). Accordingly, the most likely answer seems to be yes: Music does have a biological value. Cave paintings depicting the use of music go back 70,000 years. Flutes have been found in France dating as far back as 30,000 years. This kind of anthropological evidence hints that music making has been around a long time.

The use of instruments or voice to make sounds would appear to be a natural action. But second-guessing mother nature is always a bit risky. However, we have some clues that hint how music making might be useful. Music, vocalized or played by an individual or sung as social chorus (birds, whales, or ape choruses), may be used to attract a mate. It's likely that females might be attracted to those producing louder, better, or more pleasing sounds. In addition, it may be that music was often used for intragroup communication, which increased group safety and identification. Likely, robust vocalization improved notification of pending threat or environmental changes. Music may be used to increase harmony and social bonding among those playing it or listening to it. Music may have also contributed to changes in the brain (i.e., verbal memory, counting, and self-discipline), which may have enhanced survival.

There is increasing support for the premise that the brain has, built-in, all the necessary building blocks for the understanding, interpretation, and enjoyment of music. This is part of the evidence for establishing a rightful place for music in our lives: It may be part of our biological encoding. We may have developed areas in the brain that are specifically activated only by music as a means for enhancing the survival of our species. Amuisca—a condition in which a patient can speak, but not process music—and the opposite affliction, aphasia—when a person can process music, but not speech—suggests that our brain does have separate processing systems for spoken language and music, much like it does in multilingual speakers. So, while it's speculative to second guess the intent of nature, one can make a good case that music has a strong biological value. But where in the brain are these "building blocks"?

The human brain appears to have highly specialized structures for music: The raw materials (including tonotopic maps for pitch) have been identified and studied. Pitch is a primary feature of all sounds and is, in fact, necessary for auditory perception. As an element of music, pitch has been studied in cats, monkeys, and humans. If pitch is a built-in property of the brain, then damage to the area responsible for processing it would conceivably impair it, and it does. And in cases of a right-hemisphere stroke or seizure, timbre is also typically impaired (Samson and Zatorre 1994). The brain has an actual "frequency map" organized much like a string of piano keys. Neighboring frequency areas are located so predictably close together that it's uncanny. If you stimulate one part of the map with a frequency, an adjacent area of the cortex is activated, too (Zatorre 1988). This suggests a likelihood for built-in structures related to pitch, frequency, and tones.

When a normal brain processes sound correctly, the subject has a good chance of learning. When the brain does not process sound properly, learning problems result. Dr. Glen Rosen and Dr. Albert Galaburda with the Harvard Medical School discovered that those who have processing deficits do, in fact, have physical differences in their brain's auditory relay station. The dyslexics they've studied have fewer neurons in the part of the brain (the medial geniculate nucleus) that processes fast-changing sounds like ba, ta, ka, da, etc. This suggests that, while music making may enhance the brain's sensory systems, when the brain has an anomaly, the sound functioning deteriorates—a critical factor considering the enormous quantity of auditory information the brain must process. Typically, 30,000 bits per second of information pass from the ears along the acoustic nerve to the brainstem, and then into the primary auditory cortex.

Music is embedded in all cultures and its reputation as a universal language is well deserved. In a study by Manfred Clynes (1982a), forty Central Australian Aborigines of the Warlbiri Tribe scored high on the recognition of musical sounds of joy, love, reverence, grief, anger, sex, and hate. Their scores were equal to university students at the University of New South Wales, MIT, and the University of California at Berkeley.

Researcher Glen Schellenberg reasoned that if there was a biological basis for consonant tone pairs (as in the Pythagorean ideal), then naive listeners should be able to discern changes from dissonant (non-innate) tone pairs more easily than from the more "natural" consonant pairs (which should feel more comfortable). Indeed, the research verified this hypothesis (Schellenberg & Trehub 1996). However, while Schellenberg and Trehub's evidence is provocative, a future study focusing on musical dissonance as opposed to nonmusical dissonance would provide further important data.

If musical knowledge is experience-dependent, then one could reason that subjects with no musical exposure or background would not be able to make subtle distinctions in musical tones. But it turns out, most nonmusical adults can. In fact, even first graders can make this distinction. Contrary to our intuition, even six- to nine-month-old infants with no musical experience can demonstrate a kind of built-in musical awareness (Trehub, et al. 1984). This ability to discern dissonant music is reflected at a very early age, before any musical training can possibly occur. Such research makes a strong case for the hypothesis that music properties may be innate.

Another musical quality called melodic contour has interested researchers, and some believe they have identified specific brain cells that process it (Weinberger and McKenna 1987). Other cells in the mammalian auditory cortex have been found to process specific harmonic relationships (Sutter and Schreiner 1991). And, rhythmic/temporal qualities have been linked to a specific group of neurons in the auditory cortex (Hose, et al. 1987). The suspicion here is that nature has allocated the auditory mechanisms for processing pieces of music. Taken as a whole, this adds to our case for the biological necessity of music. But what about those who cannot hear? Did nature leave them out of the loop?

Surprisingly, musical history is full of examples of individuals who were successful in the field of music without the ability to hear. Examples of acquired deafness in composers include Beethoven, Franz, Smetana, and Vaughan Williams. And their subsequent acclaim suggests they suffered no diminution in composing talent (Hood 1977). Apparently, creating music can be a purely cognitive creative process that does not rely on hearing. Music performance with acquired deafness is troublesome, but some manage to continue to play or, at least, to enjoy attending live musical performances. But what about congenital deafness? Most schools for the deaf include marching band and choir in their curriculum (Edwards 1974). Some of these groups are so good that their live performances are in high demand. This suggests that music may be as much about rhythm and movement, as it is about tone and pitch. The congenitally deaf usually appreciate loud rhythmic music, which is often learned through visual and tactile input (Cleall 1983). It is likely that the qualities of music are always represented in the brain, but that a particular mechanism may simply inhibit the body's response to those musical qualities (i.e., to march, write music, or carry a note). Musical talent can be viewed as a listening or tactile practice: It engages the whole body and seems to persist in spite of physical obstacles.

Some suggest that even singing may be biologically based. We see parallels in nature with whales and birds. Singing develops under the same conditions as human language, with the necessity to hear vocalizations, the value of structure, and the critical period for learning. The bridge between vocalization and song may be a narrow one. Anthropologist Dr. Bruce Richman believes that singing lies part way between the vocalization (cries, sighs, etc.) and language (words, sentences, meaning, etc.). In fact, he says, singing gives cultures something that language and vocalization do not—social cohesion (Richman 1993). By themselves, these examples don't prove that singing is built into our brain, but taken in the larger context of a biological basis for pitch, melody, and harmony, it is plausible.

# Developmental Periods

Multiple brain mechanisms would need to be involved in order to support the hypothesis of a musical maturity process. So far, several brain mechanisms have been linked to developmental periods, but more research needs to be done. Clearly, history has provided us with inspirational examples of both innate and developed musical talent. Mozart made his first professional tour as a pianist through Europe when he was six and continued composing to popular acclaim for the rest of his life. While Mozart's talent *was* evident very early on, the German composer Richard Wilhelm Wagner failed to find popular success many times before being saved from professional ruin at age 51 by Ludwig II. Though Wagner eventually enjoyed some success, his musical talent *was not* as obvious at an early age. Rather, it was likely developed.

Developmental periods hint of a genetically-influenced mechanism that is mediated by environment. These developmental periods have received a great deal of attention lately, especially in relation to speech, language, motor, and visual development, as well as music-making skills. Several recent works have suggested that music learning has a critical period, which if missed, closes the doors to future musical competence. This claim is false. What is true is that the brain does have some periods in which it is more sensitive to the active development of music, and, thus, it makes sense to engage learners during these times. However, the research *does not say* that if you don't learn music as a youngster, you'll never learn it. Rather, it suggests that if you learn it later in life, it may take more time for you to reach proficiency.

There is no haphazard development to the human brain, and the use of neural space is allocated parsimoniously by nature. Neurons become committed to particular tasks by both genes and experience. Neurons that might have been engaged for instrument playing at age five will likely become engaged with some other activity. However, the brain is flexible (the phrase "plastic" is often used) at every age and can be trained to handle new skills, like music, any time. The matter is more of degree: That is, level of mastery and time involved to reach this level may be influenced by age and early exposure. There are, however, countless examples of adults who learn to play an instrument in their golden years.

# MUSIC PRIOR TO CONCEPTION

There's clear evidence of an in utero response to music. Loud sounds create the startle response (Lecanuet, et al. 1988). This creates a kind of associative learning, whereby the fetus reduces the response to repeated sounds, evoking habituation (Leader, et al. 1982). Whether or not this is appropriate for infants is another issue. And, just because an infant may recognize a lullaby, this doesn't mean it's necessary or valuable for his or her development. Disagreement exists over whether purposeful in utero exposure to music is beneficial at all.

## ON A PRACTICAL NOTE

At this early stage of research on the effects of music in utero, it may be better to take a cautious stance. There's no evidence of long-term cognitive or emotional benefits to prenatal music exposure. Protect the unborn child from any loud music. To be safe, make sure the volume played is not excessive, certainly below 50 decibels. Stick with singing, soft instrumentals, and lullabies.

# MUSIC FROM BIRTH TO TWO YEARS

At the Tallahassee Florida Memorial Regional Medical Center, a study was done to discover the impact of music on newborns and premature babies with low birth weight. Those who heard a tape of children's lullabies for one hour per day reduced hospital stays by five days; the weights normalized quicker; and stress levels were lower than the control conditions. Other studies have shown lowered stress levels in hospitalized adults exposed to music as well (Winter, et al. 1994 ).

After birth, the first orientation to music is typically the mother's lullaby. Infants are very accurate in identifying their mother's voices and songs as compared to others. Infants like upbeat, major key instrumentals at low to moderate volume at this age. The neurons in the auditory cortex are apparently highly plastic and adaptive at this stage of life. A landmark study demonstrated that when implanted early enough, cochlear auditory implants can help deaf kittens hear (Klinke, et al. 1999). This suggests the possibility that congenitally-deaf children may one day be able to develop hearing if the intervention is early enough. Can healthy infants discriminate between two adjacent musical notes without any music training? Yes, five-month-old infants can even discriminate between the smallest interval used in Western music, a semitone (Olsho 1984). In fact, infants eight to eleven months old have been shown to perceive and remember melodic contour (Trehub, et al. 1984). And, infants ages seven to nine months old can "chunk" music in the same way experienced musicians do (Thorpe and Trehub 1989).

Infants can recognize melodies independent of tempo. In one study, when the same notes were played in various rhythmic combinations, the changes of rhythm were instantly detected. Infants were able to tell the difference between two songs they had never heard before; one was normal and the other was digitally altered (Trehub and Thorpe 1989). When hearing the "mistakes" in the song, infants produced a surprised response. Another research team demonstrated an infant preference for original music versus altered versions (Krumhans and Juscyzk 1990). Although it's not very sophisticated, this skill, researchers believe, begins very early (Demany, et al. 1970).

## ON A PRACTICAL NOTE

In the first couple of years of a child's life, play or sing for them simple songs and lullabies. By twelve to twenty-four months, infants can incorporate body movement into the music. This is when it's good to demonstrate for them head nodding, clapping, and tapping. Just watch an infant respond to rhythm and you'll recognize the early stages of musical readiness. Use rhythm in your voice, and incorporate bells and xylophones. A good CD for this age is Baby Needs Beethoven. You might also experiment with Disney soundtracks, such as Snow White and the Seven Dwarfs, Bambi, Dumbo, Mary Poppins, Winnie the Pooh, and Gilbert and Sullivan music. A good book source is *All Ears: How to Choose and Use Recorded Music for your Children* by Jill Jarnow.

## EARLY CHILDHOOD MUSIC EXPOSURE

Here's an example of age-dependent changes. In musicians who use their left hand to play an instrument, there's evidence of larger cortical area in the sensory cortex that corresponds to the index finger (Elbert, et al. 1995). But those who began to play prior to age five showed the greatest changes, suggesting a model for critical periods of somatosensory development through music instruction.

Exposure to simple instruments is important, especially around age one. Such instruments might include whistles, harmonicas, drums, and xylophones. Encourage infants to *play with* you so that they have someone to emulate. Then, if you add some background music, their brains will have plenty of creative fodder. Begin exposing children to a wider variety of music by ages two and three. At this stage, they especially like folk songs, musicals, easy-to-hear pop songs, nursery rhymes, Sambas, marches, Irish jigs, Flamenco, and traditionals. This is the time to introduce children to singing. Also encourage the use of swinging, bouncing, swaying, tapping, circling, and marching to music. Try a John Philip Sousa march. Marches are great for engaging the body, mind, and emotions.

The question of when it is best to introduce music lessons to children is difficult to answer definitively. It really depends on the child's particular maturity level, interest, and inclination. At the present time, we also don't know at what age a child's brain mechanisms (those impacting music perception and cognition) are mature. In general, however, simple keyboard practice can begin as early as three. The Suzuki Method of violin practice begins at age three or four. Children at this stage may be out of tune, but this is perfectly normal. Some children are ready for kazoos; others are ready for recorders. Regardless, children need high exposure to a wide variety of sounds while the brain is forging novel neural networks. It is helpful when parents role model the playing of music, and when music playing is a social experience that is thought of as fun. By age four, when the brain's left hemisphere has had time to develop, it's smart to include a lot of rhythm games. At this juncture, children are ready for sticks, shakers, tambourines, and drums. It is important, however, to keep the music-playing atmosphere light, social, and fun. Kids love silly, wacky songs at this stage because their language skills have developed enough to decipher most of the words, and they begin to appreciate alliteration and rhyme.

# MUSIC FROM AGES FIVE TO NINE

As far back as three centuries ago, the French composer Couperin declared all children should start music by six or seven years old. Today's evidence suggests that exposure at an early age is beneficial, and the sooner the better. If one starts early, one may benefit from a lifetime of enhanced interhemispheric brain activity. MRI studies have shown that the fibers in the corpus callosum, which connect the left- and right-brain hemispheres, are as much as 15 percent wider in musicians compared to nonmusicians (Schlaug, et al. 1995b). It should be noted that this does not necessarily mean more or better interhemispheric connectivity (or generalizable benefits); however, the wider bandwidth only occurred in adult subjects who began playing before the age of eight. Those who started after showed no difference in their corpus callosum than nonmusicians. Thus, to optimize skill development, it appears necessary to start early. Consider this: None of the world-class pianists that we know of began playing later than ten years of age.

But how early and how much should we be pushing children to begin to create musically? Some evidence indicates we may be missing out on an enormous amount of talent by not encouraging student composing. Various studies have been done with children ranging from five to fifteen years old. Many teachers and composers have suggested that, when given a chance, school-age children can compose music and will produce quality work (Upitas 1992).

A rigorous study with nonmusical children ages seven, nine, and eleven years old provided some genuine insights into the processes of music composition. Each student was given a keyboard and ten minutes to compose an original work. Keeping things easy, they all started with middle C and used only the white keys. Researchers tallied the time spent on exploration, development, and practice. All were able to successfully create novel compositions (Kratus 1989). While the seven-year-olds spent most of their time on exploration, the nine- and eleven-year-olds spent more time on development and practice. This may be a result of developmental age: The older children have more frontal lobe maturation and increased bridging of the corpus callosum. This maturation allows for greater complexity and the ability to juggle abstractions.

But the most interesting part is that Kratus did a follow-up study years later; and this time he investigated the creative process of children's compositions. What he discovered was that audiation (the ability to create and hear a piece in your head) is present in nine-year-olds (Kratus 1994). This process is critical because it allows one to try out a musical possibility without actually having to compose it. In essence, your brain becomes a musical "sketchpad." This process is identical to that used by professional musicians. These findings suggest that we may be under-rating the creative ability of our students. Students like to compose and will do it if given the chance. By age nine they have the basic mental processes in place to compose—perception, rhythm, and tone. This will hopefully encourage all of us to include composition—one of the most creative parts of music—in our lesson plans.

## ON A PRACTICAL NOTE

From five to nine is a good age to begin music lessons. Every child can play an instrument. Singing is still beneficial at this age. Read poetry that is highly rhythmical like that of Jack Prelutsky and Tom Glazer. Keyboard, piano, violin, or recorders are all great instruments for early music training. Children are also ready, as they approach eight and nine, to try their hand at composing simple songs. A handy guidebook on specific music selections is *Good Music, Brighter Children* by Sharlene Habermeyer. A good CD to purchase would be one that includes a variety of musical genres. This is the time to introduce reggae, classical, romantic, hip-hop, and pop. Soundtracks to Disney movies, especially the older ones, provide exposure to classical music, romantic music, and show tunes.

Many of the compositions by the following artists work well at this stage (5 to 9 years old); however, you'll want to experiment and find your own favorites: Mozart, Haydn, Prokofiev, Ravel, Rimsky-Korsakov, and Seeger. Selected titles include Sleigh Ride, German Dances, The Scarf Dance, Whales and Nightingales, Jonathan Livingston Seagull, Variations on a Nursery Song, The Sorcerer's Apprentice, Lincolnshire Posy, Country Gardens, Story of the Little Tailor, Toy Symphony, March of the Toy Soldiers, John and the Magic Music Man, Sinbad the Sailor, Joseph's Technicolor Dream Coat, Berceuse, Gaite Parisienne, Dance of the Hours, Story of Babar the Elephant, Peter and the Wolf; Tubby the Tuba, Mother Goose Suite, and L'Enfant et les.

# MUSIC AT AGE TEN AND BEYOND

How much music mastery can an individual attain when they start at age ten? This question is difficult to answer because of the enormous variation in prior experience and exposure. If conditions are good (family history of music, music played in the environment, and the use of skills that aid development of the auditory system), however, one may still become a highly competent musician. Chances are highly unlikely that the individual will become a world class musician, but that is rarely the objective. Most adolescents or adults can become competent on most instruments with sufficient training and practice. It should be remembered that the nonmusical benefits (satisfaction, memory, creativity, relaxation, self-discipline, etc.) may be as great or greater than the more obvious skills acquired.

# Music Enhances Cognition

If music making contributes to the development of essential cognitive systems, which include reasoning, creativity, thinking, decision-making, and problem-solving, what might be happening in the brain for this to occur? Quite simply, music making seems to activate and synchronize neural firing patterns that orchestrate and connect multiple cognitive brain sites. Thus, the brain's efficiency and effectiveness is enhanced. The key systems impacted are well connected between the frontal, parietal, and temporal lobes, as well as the cerebellum. The value of music making to spatial reasoning, creativity, and generalized mathematical skills has been pretty well established, but is there a correlation between music and intelligence?

# MUSIC AND IQ

The birth frequency of truly musically gifted individuals or musical savants (with mental retardation) is low: Less than two dozen cases are recorded in the literature. Most evidence suggests that even musical geniuses devote extraordinary efforts to their pursuits (Obler and Fein 1988). The reverse condition, highly intelligent individuals with no musical talent, has not been well studied; however, it is generally accepted that between five and ten percent of the population cannot give baseline performances on rudimentary musical tasks such as singing a simple well-known song or tapping to its beat. One could gather from this that musical and generalized intelligence are probably not related.

But there's more to the puzzle. When you consider that students at the world's top music academies have an average IQ of 130 (Jourdain 1997), a correlation might seem obvious. These students, however, are not randomly admitted. Although many musicians do, in fact, have an above average IQ, many are quite ordinary. And, although some research suggests the music-IQ connection, the links are typically specific to spatial and hidden pattern tests and have gender variations. Overall, the studies are mixed. One researcher argues that participation in a variety of music activities helps us acquire six distinct levels of cognition including perception and judgment (Serafine 1988). One problem in making findings about the impact of music on the cognitive systems is obvious—there is a wide range of abilities along the continuum of musical skills between novice and expert. So, where does one begin to measure differences? Measuring the impact of music on cognition is fraught with biases and difficulties. First, while it is not practical to use invasive methods to study the human brain, neuroimaging devices, such as EEGs, ERPs, PET scans, and fMRIs have been helpful (Hodges 1996). But then the question arises, "At what age should we try to evaluate the brain?" And then there are an enormous number of potential subgroups (i.e., perfect pitch versus musicians without perfect pitch). In spite of all this, there are some emerging and important discoveries.

# OUR NEURAL SYMPHONY

Many have suggested the actual mechanics that might support a brain theory to explain how music enhances cognition. Canadian psychologist Donald Hebb's 1947 insight that synapses and neural networks are at the core of learning was pivotal. By 1954, physicists Cragg and Temperly introduced cooperative state phenomenon, which suggests that the interaction among particles in a system can allow a huge number of behaviors to be produced. In the mid-1970s, physicist William Little's mathematical model for superconductivity allowed us to predict the behaviors of atoms. And, in 1985 Vernon Mountcastle introduced the columnar organization principle of the cortex. What was left was to integrate all of these puzzle pieces into a single coherent hypothesis that related music and cognition.

University of California, Irvine, physicist Gordon Shaw has been one of the most vocal supporters of a hypothesis of neural synchrony (Shaw 1978, 1983, 1988, 1993, 1998). Briefly, the theory states that the activation between family groups of cortical neurons assist the cortex in pattern recognition. This multiple-site, cross-activation may be necessary for higher brain functions including music, cognition, and memory. While not universally supported, this basic theory of neuronal ensembles is gaining support from others in relation to other sensory and motor areas (Barinaga 1998; Calvin 1996; Fries 1997; Riehle, et al. 1997; and Stopfer 1997).

Thus, it may be that built-in cortical repertoires of patterns and their sequences are the building blocks for understanding, appreciating, and engaging in music. These patterns should show some relationship to the specific effects of music, and they do (Sarntheim, et al. 1997). Taken as a whole, these puzzle pieces form a plausible theory, which suggests how music may have a fast track to engaging and enhancing higher brain activities.

*Music Activates Multiple Sites*

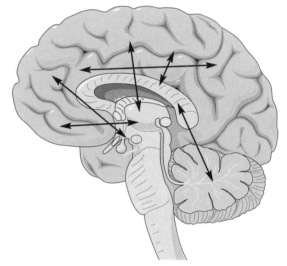

If this theory that music might be inducing more activity among all areas of the brain (known as "coherence") is correct, then it would follow that females would have greater EEG coherence, since they have more interhemispheric connections, particularly in the anterior commissure (Allen and Gorski 1991). And, it turns out that this is true. In one study, researchers found that indeed musicians had far greater coherence than nonmusicians, and females had higher coherence than males (Johnson, et al. 1996). This suggests the possibility of a reorganization of brain activity that influences cortical connectivity enough to disperse neural firing over a larger area, and at the same time, connects brain areas.

A Russian study (Malyarenko, et al. 1996) suggests that listening to music even one hour per day changes brain reorganization. An experimental music group of four-year-olds were exposed to classical music in the background for one hour each day. Subsequent EEG readings suggested greater brain coherence and more time spent in the alpha state. This body of data hints that music does influence not just brain activity, but coherence. This may be the neural symphony that Dr. Shaw has proposed. Since different types of music do different things to the brain, highly complex music may increase wide areas of coherence, whereas simpler music may have other important benefits.

## MUSIC AND MATH SKILLS

The traditional associations of math and music hint that perhaps there is an overlap in neural connections to these relative areas of the brain. Using behavioral and neuroimaging techniques, researchers have uncovered the most common areas activated during mathematical operations. The key math areas of the brain, it turns out, have some overlap with areas highly involved with music. Research with both stroke and brain-diseased patients suggests that several areas including the frontal, parietal, and temporal lobes are at the core of our math skills. This discovery begs the question, does music learning enhance math? Or is it the math that enhances music? Cognitive scientist Howard Gardner believes musical talent is built-in (Gardner 1983). Right now, the evidence is leaning in his direction.

*Primary Math Areas*

*Primary Musical Areas*

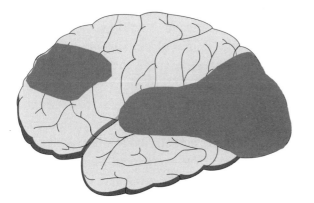
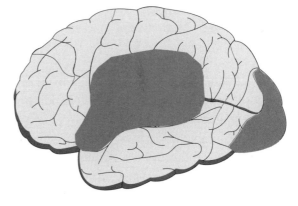

Dr. Shaw's group did an interesting experiment to find out the impact of music on math. If music impacts our ability to understand proportions, math scores should improve with music exposure. So he designed a study that compared the following three groups of second graders:

◆ Twenty-nine students received piano instruction and a math video game.
◆ Twenty-nine students received computer-based English training and a math video game.
◆ Twenty-eight students received no piano instruction and no video (control group).

*Music Helps Math*

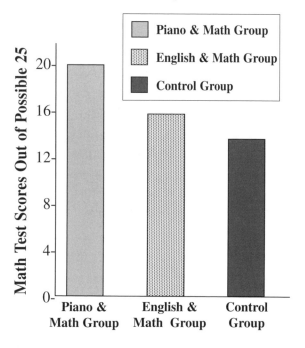

The results were impressive (Graziano, et al. 1999). The math video game, designed by Shaw to increase spatial-proportional skills, boosted math scores by 36 percent in both experimental groups. But the group that also took piano lessons scored an additional 15 percent higher than the other experimental group, which received no music instruction (see graph at left). Shaw believes this demonstrates that the piano playing strengthened the spatial awareness plus the ability to think ahead—both important math skills. It should be noted, however, that this increase difference may have been due merely to the extra attention that the piano instruction group received. Thus, additional research is needed.

These are statistically significant results. But let's take a different approach. Instead of testing for math effects from exposure to music, what happens when we increase time on music instruction at the expense of time on math? Dr. Spychiger of the University of Fribourg in Switzerland authored a study that addressed this question. Her student subjects ranged in age from seven to fifteen years old. Half of them were exposed to daily forty-five-minute music lessons (5 days per week), while the other half (the control group) continued to get their usual one music lesson per week. Surprisingly, the experimental group, who took a curriculum that increased music instruction at the expense of language and math, actually had improved language and reading scores (Overy 1998). In fact, they did as well as those students who spent more time on mathematics but had no music instruction! In addition, the study reports that the students with a heavier music curriculum became more cooperative and exhibited better social skills. The study, which was conducted over a span of three years, suggests music lessons may have significant long-term value.

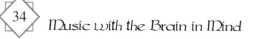

University of California, Los Angeles professor James Catterall wanted to examine the relationship between music and overall academic achievement. In particular, he was interested in determining how music lessons might impact eighth- to twelfth-grade students of lower socioeconomic status (SOLSS). His study, which compared a group of SOLSS receiving music instruction with a control group, showed a significant increase in experimental group math scores. But just as importantly, reading, history, geography, and even social skills scores soared by 40 percent, as well. Music making not only supports the development of math skills, but of all skills, for all kinds of students (Catterall, et al. 2000).

## ON A PRACTICAL NOTE

So the question then becomes, how much time should we devote to music instruction in school? The answer is uncertain, but early indications are that a good starting place is to provide lessons three or more days a week for at least thirty minutes a day. The optimal goal would then be a sixty-minute lesson each day, five days a week.

## A BREAKTHROUGH STUDY

Increased scores in spatial-temporal reasoning ability, which is considered a key building block for higher math skills (specifically geometric and topological), was the subject of a well-publicized experiment with seventy-eight preschool children in Southern California. The group of ethnically diverse boys (42) and girls (36) were pre- and post-tested and found to be in the normal intelligence range. They were also screened for prior musical background. The study was conducted over a two-year period and involved either one or two lessons per week, one hour a day. The four conditions were piano keyboard lessons, computer

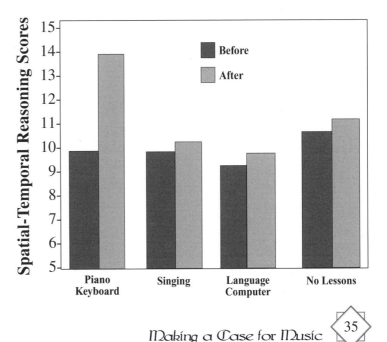

*Long-Term Value of Music Training*

training, singing, or control group. The control group continued their normal school activities with no addition of the other three activities. Professional music and computer instructors were involved. The computer lessons avoided any potential confusion with the spatial or perceptual motor aspects of the keyboard by eliminating a mouse or any software music. In a way, the singing group served as a second standard (control) because the children had prior singing experience. The results of the experiment were revealing.

On tasks of spatial-recognition (selecting from a group of options to match one object with another), the four groups performed fairly equally with no significant improvements. In fact, the small improvements were made by the singing and the no-lessons groups. But in the area of spatial-temporal reasoning (object assembly), the results were dramatic (see graph on previous page). The keyboarding group produced a significantly higher score (up to 30 percent), well outpacing the other three groups (Rauscher, et al. 1997). Studies found that the skill was present three days after experiment extinction, but others believe that long-term follow-up and continued music practice may be important to maintaining the benefits.

As we listen to music, the features of it parallel many highly complex brain functions that are necessary for memory, word sequence, and visualization. Music often has a rhythmic or rhyming quality, making it easier to remember. It is, of course, sequenced, which encourages us to try to recall songs we like, thus engaging memory. It can also become a soundtrack for what we see or visualize. (Glausuisz 1997). As a result, we can say music enhances the ability to create, maintain, transform, and relate complicated mental representation. This is done with and without sensory input or feedback. And while there are specific areas where there is more activation, all higher cognitive abilities use a wide range of cortical areas. The following represent at least four reasons why music may be activating and improving spatial-temporal reasoning and proportional math skills:

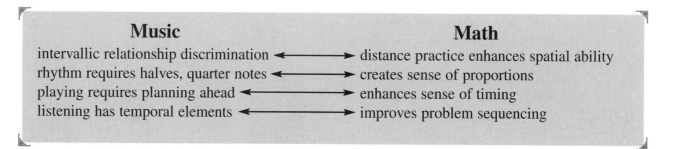

| Music | Math |
|---|---|
| intervallic relationship discrimination ⟷ | distance practice enhances spatial ability |
| rhythm requires halves, quarter notes ⟷ | creates sense of proportions |
| playing requires planning ahead ⟷ | enhances sense of timing |
| listening has temporal elements ⟷ | improves problem sequencing |

It appears that some music training can produce long-term modification in the right prefrontal and left cortical areas. The value of this study to educators is that it speaks to the tasks of learning proportions in mathematics. In fact, interviews with mathematicians suggest that music often leads to the higher brain

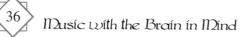

function typical of math. Possibly the structured neuronal firing pattern elicited by music strengthens the proportionalities of precise pattern-making structures necessary for the spatial-temporal skills of math. Because the understanding of proportions and spatial reasoning is essential to math skills, it's easy to see how music became the "math booster."

# WHAT IS THE REAL EFFECT OF MOZART?

In 1993, the publication of a letter in the respected journal *Nature* began a storm of controversy. In the University of California, Irvine, study, students used headsets to listen to either white noise, relaxation music, or Mozart for ten minutes. Afterwards, the Mozart group performed better on spatial tasks than those in the other two groups (Rauscher, et al. 1993). Could this be possible? Might listening to Mozart make you smarter? Although no one disputes that music has a powerful effect on our lives, the claim that it increases intelligence raised some eyebrows. The following highlights, however, reflect the real results:

## *Evidence that Supports the Mozart IQ Effect*

◆ The effect is cross-species: It occurs in rat brains, too. This suggests that it's not a culturally-driven or preconditioned-bias response (Rauscher and Shaw 1998).
◆ The effect occurs in epileptics: They, too, experienced improved spatial reasoning. This confirms the claim, essential to the theory, that music impacts neural firing patterns (Hughes, et al. 1998).
◆ In twenty-six of twenty-seven studies that have attempted to duplicate the original study, at least some positive "Mozart Effect" has been reported.
◆ PET studies suggest that Mozart sonata K.448 created significantly more signals in the frontal cortex (versus auditory cortex) than controls (Muftuler, et al. 1999). This suggests that the effect is oscillating across the brain as researchers predicted.
◆ The effect occurs in preschool children suggesting no musical talent is required, and it doesn't have to be Mozart (Rauscher, et al. 1997).
◆ EEG studies in which subjects listened to Mozart, then attempted a spatial-temporal task, showed enhanced synchrony of neuronal firing activity of the right frontal and left temporal-parietal areas when compared to a control group that listened to a short story.

## *But many questions remain:*

◆ Why have some studies failed to duplicate the statistical significance of the original Mozart findings?
◆ Why were the subjects not given listening tests first?
◆ Would longitudinal (multi-year) studies validate the long-term duration of keyboard training effects?
◆ How is this effect impacted by sensitive developmental periods for music?

- Why listen to piano sonatas, instead of violins, which produce a higher, more influential effect on the vestibular system?
- How do we know that there isn't a "Beethoven Effect" or a "Miles Davis Effect" or a "Gershwin Effect"? Why only Mozart?
- Other researchers suggest that improvement in spatial-temporal reasoning may not be the result of Mozart at all, but of the object rotation that happens to be the subset of the Mozart K.448 Effect.

Adding to the "Mozart Effect" controversy, former Georgia governor Zell Miller established a novel program in which all newborns in the state (which averages more than 100,000 a year) were to go home with a classical music CD or tape. He was quoted as saying "No one doubts that listening to music, especially at a very early age, affects the reasoning that underlies math, engineering, and chess. I believe it can help Georgia children to excel" (Prokhorov 1998). Then, other public officials began to follow Miller's lead. In Florida, a program was started that mandated children receiving state aid to have at least 30 minutes of music instruction daily. Books and CDs flooded the market claiming a "Mozart-type Effect" on learning, and the ripple became a cultural tsunami.

In fact, subsequent research has determined, for example, that it is actually a subset (primarily rhythm) of Mozart's music that inacts a subset (object rotation) of spatial-temporal reasoning ability. However, even today the controversy remains. Kenneth Steele of Appalachian State University says he could not replicate the music effects on his students (Steele, et al. 1999). Many believe the jury is still out, although some positive effects have been reported for Mozart listening. The problem is, many studies showed statistically insignificant and short-term results. However, the original researchers maintain their assertion that the music does have the effects they claim.

## ON A PRACTICAL NOTE

Short-term listening can produce a temporary gain in spatial skills for up to 15 minutes after the listening. Other kinds of "primers" (not just Mozart) can also work as well (or better) to achieve the short-term spatial skills effect. For lasting gains, nothing (so far) beats music training that starts early and continues for at least a year. Keyboard (or piano) playing is the only tested instrument to date for spatial-temporal reasoning development. Other instruments may (or may not) result in the effect, but then there may be other benefits derived from other instruments. It is strongly recommended that learners begin playing an instrument while they're in school, preferably early.

A huge part of the direct value of playing music comes from gains in spatial-temporal reasoning, a building block for proportional math. Unless students master proportions and the ability to create, hold, and manipulate objects in space, they'll be stuck in the world of math by memorization, which just doesn't work amidst infinite combinations and relationships. This critical spatial-cognitive sense allows learners to progress into fields such as engineering, lasers, robotics, design, statistics, construction, art, computations, and genetics.

## ON A PRACTICAL NOTE

Do some action research with your own students. You'll only know what works best for your learners if you experiment a little. Work with another teacher or divide your class in half for the experiment. Have group one listen to a ten-minute primer, for example, while group two acts as a control. Then switch and have group two be the experiment group on a second scenario. Differ music types and compare results. Record your results. Who knows, you may be the one that discovers the next music genre for a priming effect!

# ALTERNATIVES TO MOZART

While researchers Shaw and Rauscher were touting the value of Mozart, Lawrence Parsons of the University of Texas at San Antonio's Health Science Research Imaging Center was asking a different set of questions (Parsons, et al. in press). He wondered (1) Was it Mozart, or music as such (with all of the intricate melodic, harmonic, rhythmic counterpoint patterns), or the separate components of music that created the effect? (2) Is it just musical sound or could other kinds of primers (i.e., visual ones) work too? And (3) What is enhanced visualization or mental rotation?

Studying adults, Parsons found that auditory rhythm, but not melody/harmony, enhanced both visualization and mental rotation, and that dynamic abstract visual stimuli enhanced both, as well (ibid). The results were approximately the same for auditory and visual rhythm primers as they were for Mozart. This study suggests then that either auditory rhythm or rhythmic visual stimuli can lead to short-term enhancement of mental rotation—a useful spatial-temporal skill. The study also suggests that Mozart, or music, is effective because it possesses multiple lines of rhythmic sound streams. Even nonmusical rhythms (such as rain forest recordings) were found by Parsons to produce a comparable effect, and more complex rhythmic sounds lead to even greater enhancement compared to very simple rhythmic sounds.

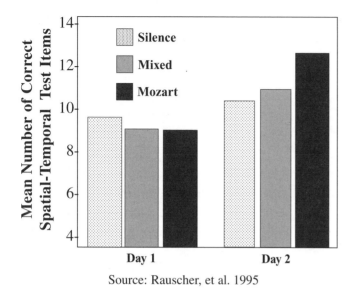

*Temporary Cognitive Enhancement from 10-Minute Mozart Exposure*

Source: Rauscher, et al. 1995

Subsequent to this landmark study, we should consider the value of matching the modality of the stimulus with the modality of the task. For example, a visual primer (like watching a screen saver full of collapsing boxes or making visual estimates of size, volume, or length) is far superior than sound alone (even listening to Mozart) if the task primarily requires visual skills (like cube comparisons). Matching a visual primer may activate and synchronize specialized neural firings, enhancing speed and accuracy in the visual areas of the brain far better than simply an auditory primer since the auditory task has greater activation to auditory areas of the brain.

## ON A PRACTICAL NOTE

The "Mozart Effect" may not necessarily be a result of Mozart (although it might work for some tasks), but related more to the fundamental building blocks of music. Various primers may work selectively on various cognitive tasks. Therefore, match learning tasks with the appropriate primer modality. For example, if the target task is auditory (like speaking a language, speeches, plays, singing, etc.) possible primers are chants and songs. But if the task is primarily visual, use a more visual primer, such as watching and visualizing. If it's more kinesthetic, use movement as a primer. Adding music to existing visual and kinesthetic primers, however, may provide more synergy, although no studies yet support this.

# MUSIC IN THE BACKGROUND

Does music in the background enhance learning performance? This is a difficult question to answer because there are so many variables including subject population, type of music, duration, length of experiment, type of learning, etc. Other confounding factors that make it difficult to study the effect of background music include individual differences in affective and stress-reduction reactions and varied synchronicity of neuronal firings in the cortex. Nevertheless, researchers have been studying these questions for a half- century. One older study of 278 eighth and ninth graders tested the effect of background music in a study hall. The experimental conditions resulted in higher reading comprehension scores when compared to the control group (Hall 1952).

In a recent study, thirty undergraduates were used with a repeated and reversed study design. This meant that the two conditions (music and no music) were repeated for the same group, then reversed so that each group got the other condition. The music used was a stress-reducing instrumental (Koan Plus software). The subjects were given a sixty-five item baseline intelligence test (AH4, Group Test of General Intelligence, Form 1) before the experiment. Then after a distracter task, the participants either heard music or silence while they took Form 2 of the intelligence test. The results were positive: Those listening to the music outperformed those in the silence condition (Cockerton, et al. 1997). No significant changes in heart rate from before to after the music listening condition were found. This suggests there was no so-called "arousal effect." It is possible that music may facilitate more focused thinking for general intelligence, not just spatial.

## ON A PRACTICAL NOTE

Music which has structural simplicity is best for background music. Consider using popular jazz instrumentals like George Benson, Kenny G, or David Sanborn. Environmental music can work wonders, too. Ocean sounds, waterfalls, and rain forest soundtracks are usually well received. In addition, baroque music, characterized by balance and predictability, can work well if it meets the following criteria: (1) It is composed in a major key; (2) It is done with orchestras, not individual instruments; and (3) The movements are adagio or andante. Other Baroque era composers whose music is predictable and balanced include Albinoni, Bach (Brandenberg Concertos), Handel (Water Music), Telemann, Vivaldi (Four Seasons), and Corelli.

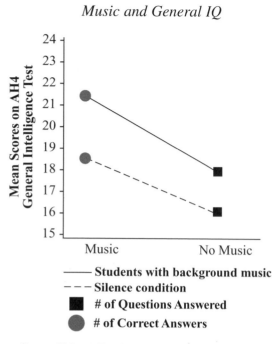

**Music and General IQ**

Mean Scores on AH4 General Intelligence Test

—— **Students with background music**
– – – **Silence condition**
■ **# of Questions Answered**
● **# of Correct Answers**

Source: Heim, A.W. 1970. *AH4 Group Test of General Intelligence.* NFER Publishing Co., Ltd.

Many preschool teachers would agree that songs, movement, and games are superb neurological exercises. Dee Coulter, Director of Cognitive Studies at Naropa Institute in Boulder, Colorado, believes strongly in the relationship between the patterns found in music and those necessary for proper neurological development. She's found that the combination of auditory and kinesthetic stimuli and teaching approaches make for strong development in language, social skills, self-management, and internal dialogue (Coulter 1995).

One study assessed whether there is melodic and rhythmic retention differences when learners are presented with visual versus auditory versus kinesthetic versus multimodal approaches. Sixty-one preschoolers ages four to five were tested before and after being exposed to one of the four experimental conditions. The subjects in the visual group saw cue cards that provided music background information; the auditory instruction consisted of singing and listening; the kinesthetic group moved to the music; and the multimodal group was exposed to all three conditions. The auditory and multimodal groups outperformed the visual and the kinesthetic groups; and the multimodal group outperformed the auditory group (Persellin 1993).

# CREATIVITY AND MUSIC

In order to be creative, many processes need to occur. First, you need the background or "mental stockpile" of information to generate ideas (memory function); then the idea itself (random or spatial-orient ideas may be a right hemisphere function); then you need a rationale (the analytical left hemisphere tends to have an interpretive function). The enhanced cortical-firing model presented earlier suggests that the brain normally moves between sequential and spatial (left and right hemisphere). Music can enhance this cross-lateral activity. Specific neuromodulators (possibly serotonin and dopamine) are involved in this creative process. The creative "zone" is a delicate mental state requiring specific thought processes and both left- and right-hemisphere dominance. Music can enhance the length of time in this zone, and, therefore, creativity. The worldwide use of music across all cultures to alter mind states gives credence to the potential correlation between music and creativity.

## RECOMMENDED SELECTIONS

Trumpet Concerto, Hungarian Rhapsodies, Ancient Dances and Airs, Pines of Rome, Lt. Kije, Concierto Aranjuez, Fantasy for a Courtier, Jonathan Livingston Seagull, Variations on a Nursery Song, The Sorcerer's Apprentice, Lincolnshire Posy, Country Gardens, Story of the Little Tailor, and Toy Symphony.

Artists include Liszt, Respighi, Prokofiev, Rodrigo, John Cage (Three Constructions), Duke Ellington (The Ellington Suites), Berlioz (Symphonie Fantastique), Peter Gabriel (Passion), Issac Hayes (Hot Buttered Soul), Bud Powell (The Best of Bud Powell on Verve), The Kronos Quartet (Pieces of Africa), and Beethoven (Fifth Symphony).

In addition, you might use Rhapsody in Blue, Piano Concerto in F by Rags Horn Concertos, Clarinet Concerto Indian Ragas, Concerto for Sitar Don Juan, Piano Concerto #5 (Beethoven), Etudes (Chopin), Claire de Lune (DeBussy), Piano Concerto #26 and #27 (Mozart), and Swan Lake Waltz (Tchaikovsky).

Some researchers report that creativity is enhanced by music (Adaman and Blaney 1995), but various types of music seem to impact us differently. The likely reasoning behind this is that music is highly mood dependent, and creativity usually develops over time. One study, however, found that a year of music instruction significantly increased creativity (Wolff 1979). The control class received no musical education, while the experimental group received thirty minutes of music instruction a day for one year. Both groups were tested using the Purdue Perceptual-Motor Survey and the Torrance Tests of Creativity. The results supported the value of long-term music programs versus a one time hit or miss approach, especially in the area of visual imagery—a key component of creativity (McKinnery and Tims 1995).

Many classroom teachers have found that music can induce a heightened state of creativity in some students. There's speculation that the influence of music on stress levels, or even possibly on serotonin levels (known to be involved with creative states), may contribute to this effect. A study in the *Journal of Learning Disabilities* found that creative social problem-solving among ninety-six seventh graders improved with both self-induced happy thoughts (a predicted outcome) and positive music-induced states. More specifically, the creativity to embellish potential solutions to mock social problems was enhanced by the use of music (Bryan, et al. 1998).

## SUMMARY ON COGNITION

If music enhances cognitive systems then there ought to be a theory supported by studies to establish this. And better overall academic performance ought to be observed as a result of music; right? Thus far, we've explored the neural symphony theory and shared the evidence that supports it. Now let's explore the applications. There's no causal evidence that music equals higher grades because of the tremendous number of complex school variables, but some facts deserve stating. A Rockefeller Foundation study found that music majors have the highest rate of admittance to medical school with a 66.7 percent acceptance rate. By comparison, the next closest major, biochemistry, averages a 59.2 percent acceptance rate (Campbell 1998). This either suggests that schools value music majors, or that the smarter students take music. Whichever one you pick, music instruction makes sense.

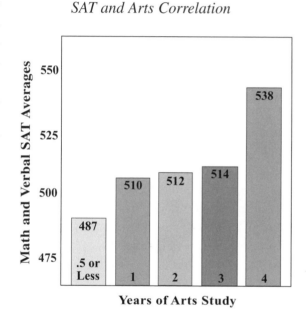

*SAT and Arts Correlation*

Studies have suggested both causal and correlative effects of music on spatial skills and reading. But how does this play out in the real world? Do all these musical enhancers add up to real-world test scores? There's a strong possibility that the answer is, indeed, yes. For example, consider that Japan ranks among the top countries in the world in math and science scores, while the United States ranks near the bottom of the list of Western countries. Are Japanese students inherently smarter? Culture is always part of the equation, but music as a component of culture, may play a role, as well. In Japan (as in other countries that rate near the top), music is a required major discipline in the curriculum, and all students receive strong music training in grades one through nine. By age fifteen, in fact, greater than half of Japanese girls have studied music privately (Stryker 1998).

There are some correlations with music and higher college entrance scores. If music contributes to cognition, more of it might lead to higher scores (up to a point). The College Board reported in 1999 that the differential between test scores of students exposed to music coursework and those who are not increases every school year. Even students who received just a half-year of music coursework averaged a 7 and 10 point gain in verbal and math scores respectively. And after four years of coursework in music performance, students averaged 58 points higher on the verbal portion and 39 points higher on the math portion of the SAT. This relationship does not represent causal evidence, but remember such evidence for raising SAT scores in other disciplines, such as English or science, does not exist either. Music making stands head and shoulders above other disciplines in its likely impact on overall learning.

# Music and Emotional Intelligence

Music may help activate the areas in our brain most involved with mood, social skills, motivational development, cultural awareness, aesthetic appreciation, and self-discipline. We know that these characteristics, sometimes called emotional intelligence, are generated out of the interplay between three systems, involving primarily the orbitofrontal lobes, parietal and temporal lobes (Wernicke's and Broca's area), and the midbrain (including the thalamic and amygdaloid structures), plus our brain's chemical messenger system (peptides). If this hypothesis is correct, there ought to be physical links between brain areas activated by music and our emotional intelligence centers.

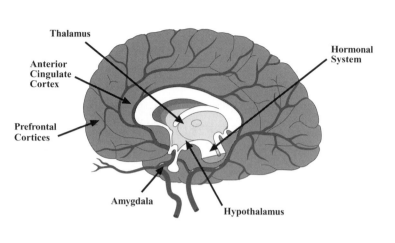

*Key Areas of the Brain That Regulate Emotion*

Thalamus

Anterior
Cingulate
Cortex

Prefrontal
Cortices

Hormonal
System

Amygdala

Hypothalamus

The emergence of emotional intelligence theory has reminded educators that the roles of cognition and emotion are intertwined. While many music supporters rightfully tout the cognitive benefits of the musical arts, the benefit package may be yet even more inclusive. Dr. Frank Wilson, neurologist at the University of California, San Francisco, says learning to play an instrument connects, develops, and refines the entire neurological and motor brain systems. He adds that learning to play an instrument is vital for the total development of an individual's brain. In short, all the systems, not just the cognitive system, benefit from music making. Thus, it should come as no surprise that music can enhance emotional intelligence.

The probable mechanism for developing emotional intelligence comes from the research on creating and maintaining neural networks. These are the complex patterns of learning that compromise our behaviors. Neural nets begin as a simple sensory activation. But neurons connect to as many as ten to fifty thousand other neurons through feedback. It has been proposed that the playing of music accelerates and enhances the ability of learners to make rapid emotional assessments and to act accordingly. While listening to music may create more moods in a shorter time, it also encourages and enhances our own mood identification. Not surprisingly, it is the playing of music (and the continuous feedback from playing) that allows music making to contribute to developing smart neural networks (Bharucha 1992). The critical elements for building the networks are challenge, novelty, coherence, time, and feedback. Each of these elements is inherent in most music making activities.

*Neural Networks Can Develop from Listening or Playing Music*

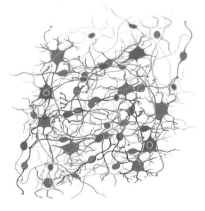

## BRAIN AREAS INVOLVED

Brain areas most involved in this development include the orbitofrontal cortex (located right behind our eyes), the thalamus, the basal ganglia (including the amygdala) and the reward pathway from the top of the brainstem to the frontal lobes. Neural networks are most prevalent in the cortex, but they do occur in significant numbers elsewhere. The musical regulation of emotional intelligence may reflect the affective response that music generates. By generating a wide rage of emotional responses, we allow ourselves to be moved by music. But it's what humans do with this feeling that counts most, and this interplay between the feelings we have and our interactions with the world is critical.

These important systems regulate a great deal of our effectiveness and satisfaction in life. And, as is often pointed out, emotional intelligence may ultimately be more important to our success than cognition (Goleman 1995), since relationships, volition, and school issues like attendance, school climate, and dropout rates are impacted. Emotional intelligence skills include the following:

◆ Identifying and labeling feelings
◆ Expressing feelings appropriately
◆ Understanding and managing feelings
◆ Controlling impulses and gratification
◆ Reducing stress
◆ Knowing the difference between feelings and actions

This high-speed path to emotional effectiveness through music making is not causal, but highly correlated in musicians and other music makers. The role of music in this area is well known. The American Music Therapy Association has been a significant force in the research, implementation, and public dissemination of knowledge in this growing field. If the hypothesis that music helps develop social skills is accurate, there ought to be studies that support the identification and development of emotional intelligence. In addition, there ought to be studies that show music can be used as a therapeutic tool. In both cases, the evidence is solid.

## IDENTIFYING EMOTIONS

Early music exposure may help children identify and manage their emotional states. Young children are excellent at interpreting emotional tones in music. In one study, children with music exposure were able to enhance the identification of emotions (Terwogt and VanGrinsven 1988). In another study, children made specific references to the emotional states elicited by the music. John Kratus at Case Western Reserve found when he tested a group of five- to twelve-year-olds (with no musical training) that they could differentiate between happy, sad, or excited emotions from Bach's thirty Goldberg variations. Consistent and accurate emotional responses to music among all children in the study were reported to begin early. With musical experience, we ought to be better able to detect and respond to emotions. Another study supports this thesis (Alexander and Beatty 1996) and suggests that music does improve emotional awareness. These studies support the hypothesis that music enhances the ability in children to detect emotions.

## ON A PRACTICAL NOTE

Music that evokes a wide range of emotions is good practice for all kindergarten through high-school learners. Try also Renaissance of the Celtic Harp, Blue Danube, None But the Lonely Heart Prelude, and Love-Death (from Tristan und Isolde). Movie soundtracks can also be effective (i.e., The Mission, Shawshank Redemption, and others).

# SOCIAL AND EMOTIONAL SKILLS

The work of Dr. Spychiger of the University of Fribourg in Switzerland is significant in that it studied seven hundred children from seven- to fifteen-years-old. The experimental groups were provided with increased music instruction, while the control group continued to receive the traditional once-per-week instructional session. The group provided with music instruction five days per week not only showed academic improvements, but just as importantly, their social skills improved (Overy 1998).

In an older study at one elementary school, music instruction was shown to enhance both social and academic skills (Farrell 1973). In a separate study, music enhanced general competence and self-concept (Morton, et al. 1998). While these are impressive results, there is still a serious lack of studies showing empirically how music impacts social skills. The likely reasons are that (1) The common bias is that music develops only cognition, so more studies focus on this area; (2) There is not one standard self-concept instrument; and (3) There is a lack of music studies in general.

Music may also aid the social skills of youngsters who are developmentally delayed or suffer from syndromes such as autism. In one important study, a group of eleven developmentally delayed children and a group of normal six- to nine-year-olds were exposed to music instruction integrated into their social play. Music was found to contribute substantially to both groups in their ability to follow directions and elaborate social play. And with the delayed children, lowered stress levels were noted possibly due to an improved ability to participate correctly (Edgerton 1994). The study reported significant improvement in CRASS (Communicative Responses/Acts Score Sheet) scores after the intervention.

Teaching students how to listen to music (for tone, rhythm, pitch, volume, lyrics, etc.) may increase their attention and focus, as well. In fact, many students who are unable to sit still and focus have hearing problems, and music may provide an excellent approach to therapy (Campbell 1998).

Self-confidence, another factor in the emotional-intelligence schema, may also be impacted by the musical arts. The Norwegian Council for Science and Humanities discovered that students who play an instrument were more likely to succeed partly because of increased self-confidence (Mikela 1990). Ask a roomful of musicians what they like most about music, and you're sure to get a few who say, "It makes me feel good—good about the day and good about myself."

# MUSIC AND BIAS

Can music be used to regulate mood, and is there any evidence of it? The answers are yes and yes. In one study of healthy adults, subjects' opinions about a neutral image changed after hearing a piece of music. Two music selections were played—one sad and one upbeat. After hearing the sad music, subjects rated the neutral images as more depressive (Bouhuys, et al. 1995). And after hearing the upbeat music, they rated the neutral images as happy. This demonstrates that the type of music one listens to, in fact, influences interpretation.

We do know music has the capacity to put all of us temporarily in "another world." These altered states are sometime broadly measured by cycles per second (cps) of brain-wave activity, categorized as:

| | | |
|---|---|---|
| ◆ | **Delta (1-4 cps)** | *deep sleep state* |
| ◆ | **Theta (4-7 cps)** | *twilight zone; half awake and half asleep* |
| ◆ | **Alpha (8-12 cps)** | *relaxed alertness; reflection; calm; prepared* |
| ◆ | **Beta (12-25)** | *busy classroom activities; discussion* |
| ◆ | **Super beta (25+)** | *intensity; drama; exercise; simulations* |

# ENHANCED SOCIAL INTERACTION

Researchers noted behaviors of twenty-seven preschool children exposed to background music. The researchers compared folk music and rock and roll to no music and observed specific behaviors, such as spatial location in the classroom, posture, and social interaction. In general, the presence of music favored greater child-to-child interactions (Godeli, et al. 1996). In another study, developmentally delayed children were successfully integrated with normal three- to five-year-olds through the use of music therapy. The music enabled youngsters to better draw out, relax, unify, and perform in social interactions. In particular the beat of the music was a key ingredient. Music contributed successfully to their engagement and socialization (Gunsberg 1991).

## RECOMMENDED SELECTIONS

The following composers/selections are excellent for evoking emotional responses: Chopin, Mahler, Stivell, Strauss, Tchaikovsky, Wagner, Nocturnes, Water Music, Lara's Theme from Dr. Zhivago, Love Theme from Exodus, Symphonies Nos. 4, 6 Verismo Arias, My Own Story, Bravo Pavarotti Scheherazade.

# MOOD REGULATION

We know that studies support the mood-enhancing effect of music, and that the effect is so powerful, people may change their opinion of visual input based on the mood of the music. In one study, a group of students and art experts were asked to view paintings while music was playing in the background. You might expect that the type of music played induced an opinion about the paintings, and, indeed, it did. What's more astonishing is that the ratings were more dependent upon the type of music played during viewing than the style and mood of the painting (Stratton and Zalanowski 1995). In short, even when a painting was rated positively prior to hearing sad music, subsequent to the sad music, the painting was rated as depressing. Many therapists, treating patients with depression, Alzheimer's, schizophrenia, and other psychological problems, have found music enhances mood and increases survival rate (Wigram and DeBacker 1999). Music, indeed, colors our world in very powerful ways.

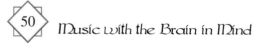

In addition, our emotive-aesthetic experience of music is important as we learn to better appreciate more types of music. Such experience can help us make distinctions in sound, tone, texture, pitch, rhythm, and harmony. We might not like every kind of music—from classical to rap, from world beat to romantic, from soft rock to heavy metal, from cool jazz to hip hop, or finally, from Tejano to baroque—but we can, with experience and training, appreciate the content and message.

## CAN MUSIC HAVE NEGATIVE EFFECTS?

The potential negative effect of certain music types on adolescent behavior has begun to concern many people in recent years. One difficulty in studying the subject is that teens who listen to heavy metal or violent rap music may already be predisposed to inappropriate behaviors. Getting teenage listeners to cooperate in such a study is also problematic. In one study involving both male and female subjects from twelve to eighteen years old, the parents were surveyed about their child's musical tastes. The questionnaires showed a strong relationship between those who listened to heavy metal and rap and lower grades, behavioral problems, early sexual activity, arrests, and drug usage (Took and Weiss 1994).

In another survey involving young male felony offenders, rap was most commonly cited as their favorite type of music (Gardstrom 1999). Narrative comments by the subjects, however, suggested that music was more a reflection of their lives than a call to action. Only 4 percent thought the music negatively influenced their behaviors, although 72 percent said that their moods were influenced by music. A separate study involving 121 high-school students suggested that although heavy metal fans espoused fewer compelling reasons for living and more thoughts of suicide, subjects claimed that the music elevated their moods (Scheel and Westefeld 1999). Although there is no evidence that listening to heavy metal causes teens to commit suicide, it does raise a red flag for potential destructive behavior. It is also possible that students with a troubled background simply may be more attracted to this kind of music.

## SUMMARY ON EMOTIONS AND MUSIC

The powerful medium of music can assist us in the creation, identification, and use of emotional states to regulate our lives. Good musicians communicate their emotions through their singing and playing, but even nonmusicians can benefit from emotional expression through music. Music making forces us to create, reflect, bare our souls, ponder, and react in new ways. When we neglect this powerful language of expression, we wither like a malnourished plant in winter. Music lets us get in touch with our feelings, our intuition, and our hopes and fears. It activates our dreams and moves us through troubled waters.

Of course, discipline is a factor in the equation. Music making forces us into delayed gratification, persistence, self-awareness, and eventually, enhanced self-concept. These life skills are absolute gold in today's global marketplace. In summary, music making enhances the systems that allow us to perceive and respond appropriately to a world rich with emotions and complex social structures.

# Perceptual Motor Systems

Music may strengthen our ability to perceive sensory information and act upon it. Hearing selected sounds, playing an instrument, and singing may improve our ability to make finer acoustic distinctions and related auditory refinements. These qualities can positively impact a variety of learning situations, especially listening and reading. The effects are a result of the physical reorganization and growth in brain areas that define and regulate these skills. Such improvement has lifelong implications, including a significant and lasting impact on our perceptual abilities.

The presence of cortical maps has been known for quite some time. These maps allow for the connectivity and coherence of neural activity. Principles of wiring and functioning are built into the maps through gene expression and experience. These self-organizing feature maps form representations of structured input patterns. For example, at an early age music activity enhances clapping and simple beating of sticks (Rogers 1990). Early studies have also shown that cortical discharge rates were highly influenced by music, setting the stage for enhancement of the sensory motor pathways (Creutzfeldt and Ojemann 1989). Pioneering researchers discovered that these physical changes in the brains of mice include increased dendritic branching, larger cell bodies, greater connectivity, and most recently, more neurons. A question comes into play, however, regarding the type of stimuli that influences these effects.

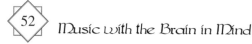

We already know that complex environmental stimuli (visual and kinesthetic anyway) impact the brains of mice in the occipital area, in the endocrine areas, the hippocampus, and overall. But might music (auditory enrichment) have the same impact? If so, the theory of neural change through auditory stimuli would be validated.

University of California, Los Angeles, neuroscientist Arnold Scheibel tells the story of an autopsy he did on a renowned

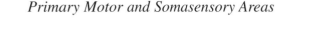

*Primary Motor and Somasensory Areas*

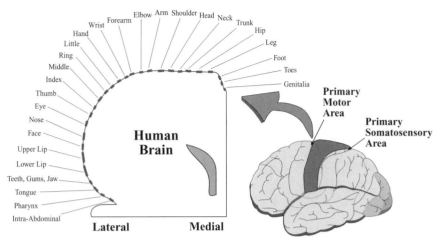

violinist. The area of the brain responsible for hearing reception (layer four, auditory cortex) was twice as thick as normal. Furthermore, a study examining the part of the cortex involved with speech suggests increased cell changes in babies with more postnatal sound exposure (Simonds and Scheibel 1989). This finding has encouraged other researchers to look for changes in the brain as a result of music making.

# HOW MUSIC CHANGES THE BRAIN

We know that with novelty, challenge, repetition, feedback, coherence, and time, the brain is enriched and new neural connections (synapses) are made. It also seems that the more one is exposed to music making, the more changes occur in the brain's neural map. Several areas are implicated: the planum temporale, the corpus callosum, the cerebellum, and the cortex. It turns out this cortical map is also impacted by the degree to which one uses his/her hands. In a study of string players, those who practiced the most had the most significant changes in their brains (Pantev, et al. 1998). Perhaps, this is nature's way of saying, "If you're going to use this area of the brain a lot, we'd better allocate more neural real estate for it."

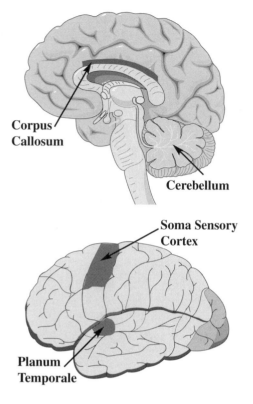

Corpus Callosum

Cerebellum

Soma Sensory Cortex

Planum Temporale

Musicians, both those with and without perfect pitch, exhibit relatively the same size planum temporale on the left side; however, the right side in those with perfect pitch is smaller than even the average musician (Schlaug, et al. 1995a). This is the area of the auditory association cortex commonly activated during music playing. So, it may be that perfect pitch is characteristic of an overall smaller planum temporale, discounting any theory that more of it makes for a better musician.

The cerebellum, another area of the brain we know to be involved in music making, especially in maintaining beat and rhythm, is also larger in musicians (Schlaug et al. 1998). When the cerebellum volume in ninety musicians and ninety non-musicians was compared, Dr. Schlaug and colleagues discovered that, on average, the cerebella of musicians was 5 percent larger than those of nonmusicians. This suggests that the many years of finger exercise derived from music playing (i.e., keyboards, horns, or string instruments) may have prompted additional nerve growth (ibid).

Among those who start music training at age four or earlier, 95 percent have perfect pitch. Among those who start music training after age twelve, only 5 percent have perfect pitch (Jourdain 1997). This suggests that perfect pitch (and the corresponding changes in the brain) *may be developed* through music training.

There is also as much as a 15 percent difference in the size of the corpus callosum in musicians versus nonmusicians (Schlaug, et al. 1995b). In musicians who use their left hand to play an instrument, there's evidence of a larger cortical area in the sensory cortex corresponding to the index finger (Elbert, et al. 1995). But the enlargement may be age dependent because those who began to play prior to age five showed the greatest changes. These and the other studies on brain changes mentioned above highlight a significant body of evidence that demonstrates that music making does contribute towards cortical reorganization.

# MUSIC AND READING

Dr. Lawrence Parsons of the University of Texas at San Antonio discovered that when musicians read music, they use an area of the brain in the right hemisphere that is normally associated with reading text. This suggests that the same attentional skills used to read words might be used in music making. In addition, music making involves the cerebellum, an area in the brain associated with movement. This relationship may reflect the spatial-movement function required for maintaining a beat. Parsons believes this finding shows more clearly than ever that music is represented in mechanisms distributed throughout the brain rather than localized in a single region (Parsons, et al. in press). Furthermore, he states there's a right-brain region for notes and musical passages that corresponds to a left-brain region for letters and words (ibid).

But what about long-term music instruction? If music enhances the development of the perceptual systems, then there ought to be correlates with tasks requiring rapid, precise perception like reading. Obviously, music making is a seeing, decoding, and problem-solving task. Thus, music training should impact one or more of the three processes involved in reading: (1) visual recognition of words; (2) comprehension, especially relating to relationships between parts and wholes—the "graphemes" and the "phonemes"; and (3) eventual visual recognition and comprehension of the wholes, without the need for the middle step.

A study involving first graders, matched for age, IQ, and socioeconomic status suggests that music facilitates reading. The experimental group of children received music instruction for forty minutes a day, five days a week, for seven months. They were tested prior to and after the intervention. The same teachers were used for both the control and experimental groups. The music group scored higher (88th percentile vs. the 72nd percentile) in both the first and second year (Hurwitz, et al. 1975). Another study suggests that music may facilitate awareness and discrimination of sounds, a key skill needed for reading (Lamb and Gregory 1993). A correlation is suggested here between how well children can read and their pitch discrimination.

There are other correlations between reading and musical abilities. Researchers at the University of Dundee in Scotland studied seventy-eight boys and girls (whose average age was eight) for abilities in vocabulary, reading, spelling, and musical skills. They discovered a statistically significant correlation between reading and spelling ability, and the ability to detect rhythm. A six-month follow-up study to determine if this relationship was causal involved two groups, one for control. The experimental group was exposed to music skill instruction in visual, auditory, and motor areas. The control group received instruction in discussion, narrative, and storytelling skills for the same length of time. At the end of the six months, the experimental group showed statistically significant gains (as compared to the control group) in reading (Douglas and Willatts 1994).

## ON A PRACTICAL NOTE

When exposing learners to music while text is being read, choose selections that match the emotional intensity and pacing of the text. If you are simply playing background music, however, keep the volume low and choose selections that are highly predictable, thus, not distracting.

## RECOMMENDED SELECTIONS

Four Seasons, Spring (Vivaldi), Water Music (Handel), Breezin' (George Benson), Brandenberg Concertos (Bach), Eine Kleine Nachtmusik (Mozart), Music for Accelerated Learning (Halpern), Environmental music (Natural Sounds), and Hot Buttered Soul (Issac Hayes).

# SOUNDS AND BEHAVIOR

Rhythmic intervention is another tool that suggests that brain's auditory system may regulate behavior. More recently, research conducted by two neuroscientists, Michael Merzenich of the University of California, San Francisco, and Rutger's Paula Tallal, has confirmed that this early model of cortical reorganization through altered auditory input can, in fact, improve reading skills (Tallal, et al. 1996). We find many types of problems associated with poor listening skills in school.

- ◆ Short attention span
- ◆ Poor impulse control
- ◆ Poor organization

- ◆ Misinterpretation of sounds
- ◆ Poor reading and vocabulary

In studies involving autistic children, when subjects were exposed to low-volume rhythmic drumbeats for an hour per day over many weeks, their behavior improved. The theory behind the rhythmic drumbeats is simple: The body and mind tend to synchronize with surrounding beats. In a brain-damaged adolescent, therapists were successful in improving speech patterns with a strong rhythm (Cohen 1988). Rhythm may be an important factor in the regulation of actions, especially in those with impulse dysregulation. When students play any musical instrument, even drums, they learn to listen.

## On a Practical Note

Introduce learners to drum rhythms. Expose them to world beat, such as the music of the Trinidad and Tobago Steelbands, African drumming, and Japanese drumming, such as performed by Soh Daiko. The Grateful Dead's drummer has released a recording called Planet Drum. Other favorite selections include Drums of Passion: The Beat by Babatunde Olatunji and The Big Bang, a 3-CD set on the Ellipsis Arts label. Ideally, students should have the opportunity not only to listen to drumming music, but to actually drum themselves. A variety of implements can be collected for the purpose of drumsticks, such as chopsticks and paint-stirring sticks. For drums, anything from the real thing to cardboard boxes or buckets will give learners the learning effect.

In a study involving nineteen students identified as ADD (attention deficit disorder) or ADHD (attention deficit hyperactivity disorder), a disorder characterized by selective inattention and impulse control problems, researchers found that subjects exposed to Mozart listening and feedback sessions (three times a week) exhibited improved focus, mood control, and social skills. Equally powerful was the fact that 70 percent of the experimental group maintained the improvements after six months, suggesting long-term positive effects (Pratt, et al. 1995).

## VISUAL AND MOTOR ENHANCEMENT

Multiple studies suggest that music playing activates high levels of sensory activity in the brain. In one study involving fifty-eight children from three to six years old, half of the subjects received Suzuki music instruction for four months and the other half (the control) received no music instruction. Four months after the intervention, both groups were tested for visual-motor skills, and the experimental group scored *higher*. This result may indicate a solid transfer effect from the music instruction.

Another study, published in *The Journal of the American Medical Association*, concluded that music positively influenced the ability of surgeons to perform. The study involved fifty male surgeons, ages thirty-one to sixty-one. They were told to listen to their own choice of music while performing their normal duties. Their choices included jazz, classical, and Irish folk songs. Although this study did not separate a potential arousal effect from perceptual-motor enhancement, the results nonetheless, were statistically significant (Allen and Blascovigh 1994).

In an unpublished dissertation, K. L. Wolff (1979) found that a year of music instruction significantly increased both perceptual-motor skills and creativity. The control group received no musical education, while the experimental group received thirty minutes per day for one year. Students were tested on the Purdue Perceptual-Motor Survey and the Torrance Tests of Creativity. The results suggest the value of long-term music programs as opposed to a short-term hit or miss approach.

## MUSIC HAS A CROSS-SPECIES EFFECT

If music, in fact, precipitates perceptual-motor changes (not just cultural or psychological changes) in humans, it would follow that it might have the same effect on animals. Dr. Francis Rauscher designed a study involving three listening conditions and ninety rats to find out. The rats were exposed to either a 65 to 70 decibel recording of Mozart's K.448 (Sonata for Two Pianos in D Major), or to a Philip Glass relaxation selection (Music With Changing Parts), or to machine-generated white noise. The stimulus, a single selection played repeatedly and continuously from a cassette tape, was provided twelve hours a day starting in utero for three weeks, then post-partum for sixty days. At sixty-one days, the researchers began timing the rats' maze performance in blind trials, while recording the number of errors made.

*Maze Running as Evidence of Rat Intelligence*

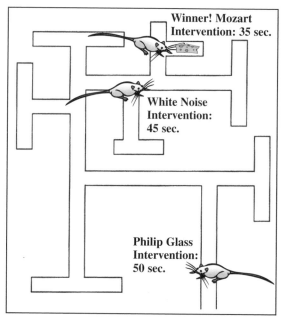

When the three groups were compared, the Mozart rats averaged 35 seconds with 2.0 errors; the Philip Glass relaxation music rats averaged 50 seconds with 2.85 errors; and the white noise group averaged 44 seconds with 3.35 errors, suggesting that the Mozart exposure improved spatial-task performance. These statistically significant differences highlight the potential positive effects music exposure may have on humans when initiated at an early age. Another implication derived from this study is that listening to music (not just playing it) may enhance higher brain function over the long haul. But, further studies are needed to determine precisely how long lasting the effect is. Even so, these results are important in that they reflect robust improvement, while controlling for prior musical exposure. Although results like these can precipitate overzealous parents to go to extremes, the good news is that no damage has ever been caused by too much soft music listening.

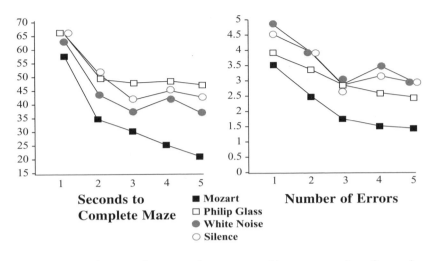

*Mozart Helps Maze Running Competencies*

**Seconds to Complete Maze**

**Number of Errors**

- ■ Mozart
- □ Philip Glass
- ● White Noise
- ○ Silence

# MUSIC, MUSCLE CONTROL, AND STRENGTH

If music impacts our sensory-motor systems, then it follows that it may also influence our muscle control and physical strength. When researchers explored this question, they discovered that different types of music do, in fact, impact strength, for better or worse. Heavy, pumping rhythmic music, they found, enhanced muscle strength, while soothing, relaxing music actually weakened it (Pearce 1981).

Many trainers now use music (combined with visualization) to regulate movement (Chase 1993) and report reduced stress, increased focus, and better performance times as a result (Brownley, et al. 1995) . Music seems to assist runners by activating skill sequences in a rhythm resulting in lowered times. Music has also been reported to improve some competitive swimmers' performance times (Hume and Crossman 1992).

Dr. Diamond adapted a test originally developed by Dr. George Goodheart, the founder of what is known as applied kinesiology, to examine the effect of music on physical strength. Goodheart's original study took a muscle and strength test that is routinely taught in medical school and modified it to provide insight into the effect of certain stimuli on the patient.

The test is eminently simple: The teacher asks the student to raise his or her left arm parallel to the floor. The tester presses down on the arm and gauges the resistance the person offers. Diamond has tested some thirty thousand different pieces of music using variations on this technique to determine whether the effect of a particular selection adds or detracts from physical strength. While some findings weren't too surprising, such as "heavy metal" exposure lowers muscle strength; others were more surprising, such as "new age" music has the same effect.

Music performance has also been found to impact a half dozen "nonmusical" skills, including internal time-keeping, fine-motor skills, and memory (Palmer 1997). Applications for these findings include a number of therapeutic interventions for auditory development. Dr. Guy Berard, a French physician, has developed a training program that treats auditory processing deficits. He says that most of his subjects have improved dramatically under his training (Berard 1993), though no peer-reviewed studies have been conducted to confirm these findings. Another company has marketed an "Earobics" program, designed to enhance auditory development and improve phonics learning. These studies and others support the belief that music can, indeed, improve a wide range of learning skills.

## RECOMMENDED SELECTIONS

Music for improved athletic performance can range from instrumentals like Rocky or Chariots of Fire to selections with strong vocals, like Flash Dance or Climb Every Mountain. Epic movie soundtracks, like the Superman Movie Theme, are always a good choice and classic guitar instrumentals, like Wild Weekend (The Rebels), Walk Don't Run (The Ventures) , Soulful Strut (Young Holt Limited), Hawaii Five-0 Theme, Triumphal March (Verdi), Persian March, Gypsy Baron, Egyptian March, and Radetzky March (Johann Strauss), and the Rackoczy March from Hungarian Rhapsody (Liszt).

 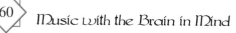

## ON A PRACTICAL NOTE

Have learners focus on how various types of music impact their body. With students divided into groups of two, facilitate the exercise described on the previous page to create awareness about music's impact on body strength. To facilitate the exercise, have one learner in each dyad stand with their left arm straight out from their side at a right angle to the body, making sure that the elbow is perfectly straight. Then have the second learner, facing the student, push down on the outstretched arm near the wrist with approximately eight to ten pounds of pressure with a firm, fairly swift action. The student should be able to resist this pressure easily. Once the students are accustomed to the standard testing techniques, ask them to take in a deep breath and hold it while the tester pushes on the outstretched arm. The tester then continues to push down at two-second intervals (while subjects continue to hold their breath) to determine if the deltoid muscle is still capable of withstanding the stress. Once a benchmark has been established, introduce music into the scenario and compare the results. Are there differences in performance? How about between various types of music?

## RECOMMENDED SELECTIONS

For greater temporary strength, use strongly rhythmic selections (for large muscle energy) and/or those that may create a strong connection or association with learners. Examples: YMCA (Village People), La Bamba (Richie Valens), Shout (Isley Brothers), Wear My Hat (Phil Collins), Un-Break My Heart (Toni Braxton), Jellyhead (Crush), Middle Eastern Belly Dancing, Samba dance tracks, Quad City DJs, Donna Summer CDs, The Best of Chic (Chic), and In the Mood (Glen Miller Orchestra).

## SUMMARY ON PERCEPTUAL-MOTOR ENHANCEMENT

For most of us, the emerging role of music represents a real paradigm shift—the notion that listening to or making music is not just for fun, but that it can also boost performance, heighten motivation, and help one attain mastery both cognitively and physically. The systems that are enhanced by music seem to be numerous, from reading, perception, and motor skills to hearing, behavior, and muscle strength.

# Music and the Stress Response

music modulates our body's stress response, thereby, strengthening our immune system and enhancing wellness. If this position is valid, there ought to be an identifiable mechanism that connects the hearing of sounds directly to our sympathetic and parasympathetic nervous systems. In addition, there ought to be studies that show alterations to the body's typical immune response agents (i.e., cortisol, ACTH, norepinephrine, etc.) as a result of music. And finally, music ought to impact blood flow. Each of these subsystems (autonomic, immune, and vascular) is critical to our health, and strongly influences the learning behaviors of our students.

## THE MIND-BODY PARADIGM

The basis for this hypothesis, that music can enhance the brain's immune and stress response system, comes from the combined work of several neuroscientists; but first, the mind-body, emotions-mind, and health-body paradigms had to be developed. These paradigms, now generally accepted, have a solid foundation of research supporting them. Psychologist and philosopher William James in the early 1900s was an early supporter of the mind-body theory which proposed that a strong connection existed between our mind and body with one influencing the other. More recently, Dr. Candace Pert in her book *Molecules of Emotion* (1997), contributed the important concept of "brain bits" circulating throughout the body. Dr. Michael Gershon contributed the notion that our "gut" is a second brain, strengthening the mind-body paradigm (Gershon 1998). Dr. Robert Sapolsky

*Sympathetic/Parasympathetic*
*Stress/Distress Response System*

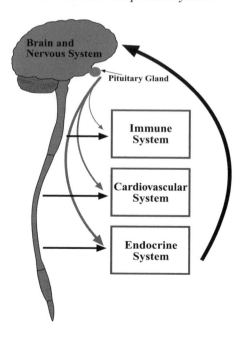

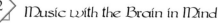

further noted that how we feel impacts our brain and health: Chronic stress kills neurons and dysregulates our immune system (Sapolsky 1992).

But the most support for the theory that music helps regulate our immune system comes from a wide range of pioneers in a variety of fields. Some of these include neurologist Oliver Sacks, Dr. Ronald Price, musician Kay Gardner, physician Alfred Tomatis, cardiologist Larry Dossey, and musicologist Don Campbell. Each of these practitioners understood intuitively the connection between music and healing. Most of them drew from personal experiences in which music helped heal those around them. But still, testimonials are one thing and evidence is another. What is the biological explanation for music's healing power?

## GOOD VIBRATIONS

While the exact mechanism is not known at this time, a plausible model exists. First, just as music has its own rate of vibration, the human body does, too. It may be that the body emits normal vibrations when well, and aberrant vibrations when sick. Music may be one way to help the body get back in synch. The human body *emits and responds* to sounds and vibrations, from the macro to the micro level. When in a natural state of rest, the body vibrates at approximately eight cycles per second. This corresponds with the alpha brainwave state, as well as with the fundamental vibrating rate of the earth itself. Vibration rates might reflect not only our general health, but our emotional state, as well.

Why this may be important is reflected in our brain's attentional, cognitive, sensory, and memory systems. Since consciousness works as a neural symphony requiring all the "bit parts" to come together, and since most areas of our brain receive and transmit information from all other areas of the body, the old distinction of mind and body or brain and body as separate is outdated. Rather, one continuous feedback loop circulates information throughout the mind-body system. Every bone, muscle, organ, and gland in this system creates and absorbs sound radiation. Our bodies, in fact, might be called "bio-oscillators," since at our very core we are composed of, and are emitting, continuous sound vibrations.

Every function in the human body has a modifiable, but basic rhythmic pattern and vibratory rate that impacts our nerves through sound. And, auditory nerve roots are more widely distributed and possess more extensive connections than those of any other nerves in our body. As such, music affects digestion, internal secretions, circulation, nutrition, respiration, and immune response through these connections. Because the human body is maintained through rhythmic vibration, it follows that musical manipulation of vibratory rates, changes in harmonic patterns, and arrangements of tonal sequences and rhythmic patterns might affect physical and mental health.

In addition to this potential health influence of vibration through music, the ear is a funnel for the sounds that hit our eardrum, connect to our cochlea, then to our vestibular. These structures move auditory input along pathways that eventually influence our thalamus (which regulates incoming sensory stimulus), hypothalamus (which is our thermostat), and the vagus nerve, which projects to our circulatory, respiratory, and gastrointestinal systems. All of these structures play a part in our health.

# MUSIC AND OUR IMMUNE SYSTEM

Given the fast pace and busy lifestyle of today's learners, the potential of music to alter moods and reduce stress is a benefit of immeasurable value. This is especially true in light of the fact that our moods influence our immune system (Bartrop, et al. 1977). We know music-induced emotions strongly impact our stress system (Rein and McCraty 1995). And, studies suggest that music can enhance the immune system responses through lowered heart rate (Blood and Ferriss 1993), as well as increase parasympathetic activity (McCraty, et al. 1996). Although too many variables exist to quantitatively compare the stress levels of musicians versus nonmusicians, we have all used music to calm us down, so we know intuitively that it can clearly act as a stress reducer.

Additionally, studies have demonstrated that music, along with other related agents, can decrease levels of the stress hormone cortisol and can increase interleukin-1, an immune booster (Bartlett, et al. 1993). Music has also been linked to system strengthening of cell-mediated immunity (Rider and Achterberg 1989), as well as humoral immunity (Rider and Weldin 1990). Another study demonstrated that children exposed to music, singing, and instrument playing exhibited increased antibodies (Lane 1992).

A study of surgery patients demonstrated that subjects exposed to music had lower cortisol levels during surgery than the non-music control group (Escher, et al. 1993).

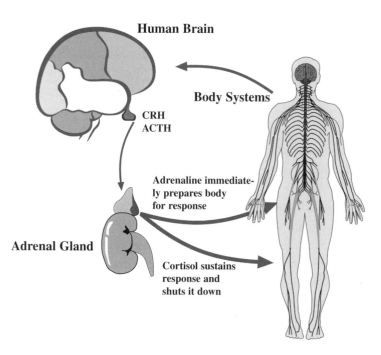

*Stress Response System*

Human Brain

Body Systems

CRH
ACTH

Adrenaline immediately prepares body for response

Adrenal Gland

Cortisol sustains response and shuts it down

Another group of patients was informed that they were going to need surgery the next day, commonly a very stressful announcement. This event generated a 50 percent elevation in cortisol levels. In the hour after the announcement, half heard no music and half heard relaxing music. The experimental group who heard music showed a much lower level of the stress hormone cortisol when measured an hour later (Miluk-Kolasa, et al. 1994). These, along with other well-designed studies, make a strong case for music therapy.

# MUSIC AND RELAXATION

Music "therapy" has emerged in the past twenty years as an aid for stress reduction, but how does it work? Apparently, the brain responds to music in the same way it does to calming words or massage. In one study, thirty-minute music sessions were given to twenty male Alzheimer's patients five times a week for a month. The melatonin concentration in serum blood levels increased dramatically and remained high at a six-week follow up (Kumar, et al. 1999). Other neurotransmitters (brain chemicals), such as nor-epinephrine and epinephrine levels were raised during music therapy but returned to pretherapy levels at the study's conclusion. Again we see that music can and does impact our immune system. The fact that the melatonin level remained elevated after music therapy supports the notion of long-term immune system enhancement.

Dr. Robert Thayer, an expert in mood management, has written extensively on the subject and has conducted a great deal of research. His studies show something you may have suspected by now: Music is a commonly used and powerful mood enhancer. When asked the question, "What behaviors do you use to reduce nervousness, tension, or anxiety?" college students responded with answers such as talking to others, positive self-talk, and listening to music, in that order (Thayer 1996). Of the twenty-one potential mood regulators presented in the survey, music ranked third with only a six percent response difference between it and the top ranked mood modulator—talking to others. Clearly, we live in a culture that knows the value of music. This reduction in stress and anxiety is important because we know that not only is our

*The Impact of Stress on the Endocrine and Sympathetic Nervous Systems*

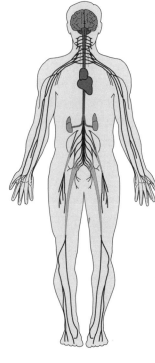

**Endocrine System**
**Higher production of cortisol:**
- **worsens heart arrhythmias**
- **increases bad LDL cholesterol**
- **spurs accumulation of abdominal fat**

**Sympathetic Nervous System**
**Higher production of catecholamines:**
- **increases blood pressure**
- **quickens heart rate**
- **thickens blood**

immune system negatively impacted by chronic elevated stress levels, so is our brain (Sapolsky 1992). Beyond cell death in the hippocampus, excess levels of cortisol are also associated with declarative memory deterioration (Newcomer, et al. 1999).

The good news, however, is that music can help regulate the body's levels of cortisol and secretory immunoglobulin A (IgA), both important indicators of health. Higher levels of IgA are associated with less frequent illness (McClelland, et al. 1980). In one study, college students were given one of four listening conditions—either radio music, tones and clicks, Muzak, or silence (control). After thirty minutes, IgA levels were measured. Of the four conditions tested, only Muzak lowered the IgA levels. This strengthening of the immune system can be helpful in two ways: First, many students arrive at school already in a distressed condition, so a brief intervention of music can move learners closer to the optimal learning state of relaxed alertness. Secondly, strengthening the immune system is especially important to learners living in suboptimal conditions that predispose them to illness.

Studies indicate that the response to particular types of music varies between individuals. College students exposed to two music selections, one considered calming and the other considered energizing by researchers, reported cross responses to the music. For example, some students rated what was considered calming by the researchers as energizing (VanderArk and Ely 1993). Interestingly enough, the researchers noted that those who rated the music as calming were biology majors and those who rated it as energizing were music majors. It is thought, perhaps, that the music students were more critical listeners than the biology students were, and as a result, their cortisol levels were increased in response to the more analytical nature of the task for them. In post-experiment interviews, the music majors reported that they were actively engaged in processing the music, some even playing the music in their heads. A prior study by the same researchers (VanderArk and Ely 1992) had uncovered this phenomenon. So the second study was designed to test the premise that biology majors may experience fewer changes in norepinephrine, cortisol, and endorphin levels in response to "calming" music when compared to music majors. And, indeed, the premise was affirmed.

It is not a wide leap, therefore, to suggest that music exposure may help regulate cortisol, steroid, and other neurotransmitter levels—physiological elements that impact mental, as well as physical health and well being. When we consider that 3 to 10 percent of school-age children are estimated to have some form of depression depending on their age, the huge upside potential of music exposure ought not to be ignored. Considering that school-age depression is a significant problem, and cortisol is the peptide that influences negative expectations, it's no wonder so many students turn to music on their own, if not through school, as a form of self-medication. Anything that helps regulate moods does not go unnoticed by teenagers!

# MUSIC AND BLOOD FLOW

An unusually high resting heart rate can indicate potential health risks, medical reports suggest. And, excess noise can raise blood pressure by as much as 10 percent. Researchers speculate that excess noise may trigger our brain's stress response, resulting in increased adrenaline levels and strain on the heart (Thaut, et al. 1991). But depending upon the music you choose, music can either calm you down or perk you up. In fact, music can impact nearly any kind of blood flow response desired. Headaches caused by weak blood flow, for example, can be aided by listening to favorable music (Epstein, et al. 1974).

In addition, music has been shown to reduce back and other postural pains in one study (Ishii, et al. 1993). The traditional view (pre-1980) that music primarily activated the right-brain auditory cortex, has been expanded. We now know that music has a more global effect on the body and is not localized to any one area of the brain.

Dr. Hellmuth Petsche of the University of Vienna says that many regions of the brain cooperate during musical activities like composing or listening. He found a surprising coherence of patterns at multiple brain sites when subjects were involved in specific musical tasks (Petsche 1993). While nonmusicians do, in fact, seem to process music in the right frontal area of the brain, harmony is processed on the left side in the fusiform gyrus. Rhythm is processed in both the basal ganglia and the cerebellum. Melody is processed on both sides in the fusiform gyrus. And, tonal processing is lateralized to the right temporal cortex (Zatorre and Samson 1991). It should be noted that these specialized areas are simply experiencing *more* activation, but are not the exclusive domain of the involved task. Other areas of the brain are activated as well, but to a lesser degree.

*Major Arteries in the Brain*

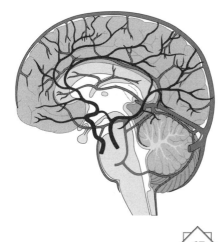

In a German study, Doppler ultrasound measured heart rate (left ventricular diastolic behavior), arterial blood pressure, ACTH levels, and adrenaline levels of subjects exposed to three types of music. The music selections consisted of a rhythmic waltz (Strauss), a non-rhythmic piece by a modern composer (Henze), and a highly rhythmic selection by an Indian artist (Ravi Shankar). Of the three, the Ravi Shankar selection was rated by the researchers as the highest in musical predictability, and results showed that only the Ravi Shankar selection reduced cortisol and noradrenaline levels (Mockel, et al. 1994). While two of the three music selections had strong rhythm, factors distinguishing the Ravi Shankar music was less melody and tonal variation, and more predictability. This finding suggests that music "across the board" doesn't elicit the arousal effect. Rather, it varies with type of music.

## MUSIC INCREASES STRESS

Music can also *increase* stress levels. Such an effect might be desirable if, for example, you want students to get supplies and materials put away before the bell rings. Just the right music can help elicit the body state that motivates people to act, move, or do something rapidly. In one study, runners were exposed to high-intensity music, low-intensity music, or no music (control) following high-intensity exercise. The group exposed to the high-intensity music experienced increased levels of stress hormones, while the other two conditions showed no cortisol changes (Brownley, et al. 1995). Evidence suggests that such a response to high-beats-per-minute music may be universal! This is great if an adrenaline response is what you desire. It's another matter all together, however, if what you desire is the optimal learning state of relaxed alertness.

In one experiment, techno-pop music increased the stress hormones cortisol, ACTH, norepinephrine, growth hormones, beta endorphins, and epinephrine, in addition to the expected increases in heart rate and blood pressure (Gerra, et. al 1998). Interestingly, classical music in this same study showed no increase in hormonal concentrations. Nor were there any gender differences noted between the sixteen students (8 females, 8 males).

We know that music can alter vascular activity or cerebral blood flow. And we've all felt the effects of relaxing music, but how does it relax us? One of the ways is through modulation of blood flow. One study involving twenty-three healthy adolescents monitored subjects' heart rate twenty-four hours a day with a Holter-Monitor secured to their body. Each was exposed to rhythmic classical and baroque instrumentals (Bach, Vivaldi, and Mozart). The subjects, when compared to a control group, showed two changes in blood flow as determined by heart rate. The first change was a reduction in heart rate, and the second was a significant reduction in heart-rate variability (Escher and Evequoz 1999).

## HORMONES

If music is involved in endocrine regulation, there ought to be evidence of a music-hormone relationship. Data suggests that, among all the other complex factors that drive the ability of individuals to excel in music making, testosterone is a strong factor. Salivary tests indicate there is likely an optimal testosterone range for the expression of creative musical behavior. For males, lower testosterone is linked to greater musical ability, and among females, higher testosterone than normal (which is still much less than what is considered normal for males) is correlated with musical ability.

We've learned that music can help regulate stress, boost blood flow and heart rate, and strengthen the immune system. These benefits are critical because most of us have experienced an increase in student stress in the last few years. Certainly student learning is negatively impacted by chronic stress and distress, and the value of music to reduce stress, strengthen the immune system, and speed recovery is strong. However, it must be cautioned that school environments are fraught with complex variables that also contribute to immune system functioning. Threats, peer pressure, gang activity, bullying, lack of nutrition, lack of physical conditioning, neglect, abuse, and poverty, all impact learners' immune and stress responses, as well. No one is claiming that music is the magic panacea here to cure all our assorted school ills; however, many agree that it is, indeed, a powerful and underutilized influence that can make a world of difference in our students' lives.

# Music and the Memory System

There are two ways in which music may enhance the development and maintenance of our brain's memory system: (1) By activating our attentional systems, and; (2) by activating multiple memory pathways. Music does this by increasing our attention to sounds, timing, perception, while embedding emotional content. What we pay attention to is what we're most likely to remember. Second, it activates and strengthens multiple memory systems for both explicit and implicit memory. Retention and recall are improved dramatically. If this hypothesis is true, there ought to be physical evidence of it. There also ought to be studies that support the notion that playing or listening to music strengthens and enhances the ability of the listener to concentrate and perceive sensory awareness.

## ACTIVATING THE ATTENTIONAL AND MEMORY SYSTEMS

Our attentional system is regulated by the interplay of many brain areas including the frontal lobes, the lateral geniculate nucleus, the reticular formation (which surrounds the thalamus), and the thalamus. As we explored earlier, the thalamus is the "Grand Central Station" for incoming sensory stimulus. In fact, Nobel laureate Francis Crick calls the thalamus "the gateway to the cortex." This critical structure oscillates normally at about 40 hertz per second, and changes in this frequency can create instability in the organism. Any structure that relies on particular frequencies can be influenced (both directly and indirectly) by other frequencies, such as those derived from music. It is postulated that our attentional system is directly influenced by music via our ear-to-cochlea and vestibular-to-neural pathways and through absorption via our bones and skin.

Our memories are influenced by music in a variety of ways, and are encoded differently depending on the task. For example, a discussion or sight reading of music may be encoded in semantic memory, while automated responses (such as tapping to a beat) are encoded in reflexive memory. And, general music listening would be encoded in episodic memory (when and where you heard it), while learning to play an instrument is ultimately encoded in procedural memory. We may develop each of these pathways separately, which helps to explain why some areas of our memory are better than others.

In addition, there's evidence that specific elements of music, such as chords, harmonies, timbre, volume, and pitch, may evoke and train separate memory systems (Zatorre et al. 1994). The hypothesis here is that the very act of listening to and, in particular, playing music may strengthen one or more of our memory systems. While engaging our brain for prediction, analysis, sequencing, and encoding, compositions containing hundreds of notes per minute provide mental exercise of sorts, and force the brain to pay better attention to auditory input.

*Attentional System*

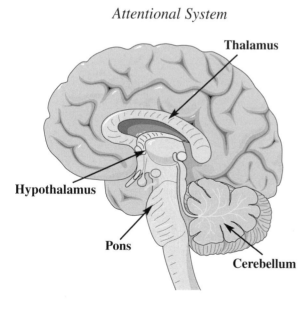

**Thalamus**

**Hypothalamus**

**Pons**

**Cerebellum**

*Music with the Brain in Mind*

# ENGAGING MULTIPLE MEMORY PATHWAYS

Memories may be either implicit (nonverbalized or unconscious) or explicit (that which we talk about or are conscious of). The implicit memories include our procedural memories such as bike riding and driving a car. They also include our stimulus response behaviors such as the "hand on a hot stove" effect. Our emotional memories from trauma to celebrations are also implicit. The written or verbal dialogues about these experiences, however, are explicit. When explanations or explorations are autobiographical, the memory pathway is episodic. It's possible for a memory to be stored in many pathways, and both explicitly and implicitly, thus increasing the likelihood of retrieval. A personal example may add some clarity.

Years ago, I was driving to my girlfriend's house for a weekly event, our Saturday night date. But this date was different—it ended before we started with an emotional break-up. The long drive home gave me plenty of time to feel sorry for myself. Hoping to find solace on the radio, my fingers froze when a particular song by Carole King called "It's Too Late Baby" played. The combination of the song (emotional trigger), with the emotional event (implicit), became embedded over time. But what also became embedded was the exact location of the incident (episodic), the feel of the Volkswagen (procedural), and the dialogue of the story (semantic). The trigger to retrieve the entire event is a simple song. This combination of elements formed a powerful memory trace in a way that other reminders, like a photo, could never do.

*Locations of Memory Activations*

**Amygdala**
(mediates intense emotional events)

**Cortex**
Temporal lobes
(semantic retrieval)

**Hippocampus**
(mediates semantic & episodic memory)

**Cerebellum**
(prodedural learning, reflexive learning, & conditioned responses)

## MUSIC AND MEMORY

The single, most consistent cluster of skills essential to musical talent may be a strong melodic memory. Because school success often requires a broad-based memory, a relationship between the two may help explain why musicians disproportionately also achieve academic success. As mentioned earlier, students who are involved in music making score higher on most measures of academic success, such as grades and college entrance exams.

Studies suggest memory may be enhanced by music instruction, and particularly when instruction begins at an early age. In a study involving sixty college students, those who had received music training before the age of twelve scored higher in tests of verbal memory (Chan, et al. 1998). But this suggests several hypotheses. Music may have enhanced memory formation by training the brain to focus on and recall extended auditory passages. Or, perhaps, the students self-selected for music training or academic prowess. So we look further. What about visual memory?

Using a movie as the visual source, students were asked to recall various parts of a film they had seen. It turns out that the soundtrack (the background music) was a significant factor in whether or not the students recalled the visual material. Music did enhance visual memory, but the question is, was it the release of hormones (i.e., adrenaline) that strengthened the recall or was it the frequency, pitch, melody, etc. of the music, and its impact on the brain that strengthened recall? This may sound like the proverbial question: Which came first, the chicken or the egg? But it must be asked. Another way to explore the question is this: Was it the visual or the auditory stimulation that enhanced memory?

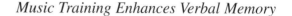
*Music Training Enhances Verbal Memory*

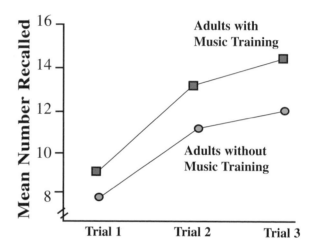

A study by Cahill and colleagues attempted to find out. Student subjects were all shown the same slide show, which did not vary in visual presentation. But in some cases, the auditory track (a vocal explanation of the slides) was changed from bland to stimulating. The students who received the stimulating sound track subsequently scored higher in memory tasks when compared to those who received the bland sound track (Cahill, et al. 1994). The question arises, however: Did the altered slide show engage stronger emotions? Or, did the stimulating audio track merely trigger more emotions, thus increasing the flow of adrenaline? Using beta-blockers, the researchers were able to control for emotions and then test recall, and under these circumstances, the positive memory results did not occur. Thus, the memory enhancement achieved in the earlier study is believed to be a result of the increased adrenaline. It is clear, however, that the sounds triggered the adrenaline, suggesting that auditory inputs may characteristically influence our memory success.

Music aids memory because the beat, melody, and harmony serve as "carriers" for the semantic content. This is why it's easier to recall the words to a song than a conversation. Put key words to music and you will typically get better recall. In a study conducted at North Texas University, researcher Dr. Barbara Stein and colleagues had student subjects review twenty-five vocabulary words. The control group reviewed their word list in silence, while the experimental group was exposed to Handel's Water music. The group exposed to music tested better than did those who reviewed in silence (Stein, et al. 1984).

Music also has the capacity to elicit memories (procedural and reflexive) and prior conditions of wellness through performance. A well-known case involving a lady known as Rosalie illustrates this point. Rosalie, who was paralyzed with Parkinson's disease, would sit depressed, immobile, bored, and listless all day long. But when provided with a piano and asked to play Chopin, a new woman would emerge. Mind-body memories revitalized, Rosalie would perform like she did many years prior as a concert pianist. And, during such performances, her EEG would indicate normal functioning (Sacks 1991). Clearly music is either evoking healthy procedural memories or changing the body's condition so that it can act healthy.

In a study involving a group of Alzheimer's patients, the subjects were able to recall more material when it was sung versus spoken. This suggests that musically embedded memories have stronger pathways or engage multiple pathways more resistant to memory loss. Patients recalled 62 percent of sung material, but only 37 percent of spoken material. And, when subjects were asked to hum or sing along with text read to them out loud, their memory of new information rose to 75 percent.

# READING, MUSIC, AND MEMORY

So, what about using music as a background accompaniment for youngsters in reading? In one study, twenty-seven kindergartners participated in a program that brought music into their whole-language-reading program. The young subjects were divided into three groups: (1) spoken text rehearsal; (2) singing text rehearsal; and (3) spoken and singing text rehearsal both. They were then tested on recall and analyzed for mistakes in substitution and omission. The two groups exposed to music exhibited far superior scores when compared to the spoken text only group (Colwell 1994). This finding supports the long-standing premise that music facilitates verbal memory.

In a study in which students were exposed to background music while learning, results suggested that matching the mood of the music to the content (such as uplifting music to positive content or depressing music to pessimistic content) resulted in enhanced memory of the material (Taniguchi 1991). And, when music induces various moods, students are more likely to pay attention to words that match that induced mood. This may help explain why we tend to better remember words that are congruent with their music accompaniment, such as movie soundtracks.

*The Brain's Primary Reading Areas*

**Visual Area**

**Frontal Lobes**

**Wernicke's Area**

**Temporal Lobe**

Another study suggests that music seems to aid in the understanding and transfer of knowledge (Reeves and Weisberg 1994). Music improves the spatial learning transfer in ways that suggest learners may be able to solve related problems (McFarland and Kennison 1998). There may be a carry-over from music instruction to reading skills, as well (Benson, et al. 1997). Interestingly, listening to Mozart music triggered activation in different cortical areas, not just the auditory cortex where we would commonly expect activation. In fact, it has been shown to activate the same area of the brain that "lights up" when we're using our working (short-term) memory. This may help explain why memory is often enhanced when music is involved.

Music may stimulate the low-frequency theta range of 4 hertz, which is absolutely critical to the encoding of information by the hippocampus for later distribution to the cortex.

# IMPLICIT LEARNING AND MEMORY

Another value of music may be the type of memory pathway it engages. Jay Dowling, a music researcher, designed an experiment in which the correct response was too fast for normal, conscious declarative memory to process. The only way subjects could identify the correct response was to rely on their instant-quick procedural memory, which we use instinctively when there's no time to think before reacting. In his study, the procedural responses were found to be quite fast and accurate (Dowling 1993). This finding holds implications for learning efficiency.

Dowling believes that too much of our schooling is based on the declarative system, a much slower memory pathway. A straightforward music education program may enhance our procedural learning system—a much faster memory pathway. The procedural system which induces the brain to develop a standard fast pattern schema, is stored in our superior long-term memory. The more educators use music to assist in the learning of other material, the more quickly and accurately the material will become embedded. Instead of relying strictly on lecture, educators who use more movement, singing, and music will improve learning efficiency and retention.

In a study of nonmusicians, subjects were divided into three groups (one control). While one experimental group learned about music passively with visual aids, lecture, and examples (declarative memory), the other one was taught through singing, clapping, and moving, but no lecture (procedural memory). After five weeks of instruction, all three groups were tested. Surprisingly, both of the experimental groups did equally well as reflected by test scores, while the control group tested poorly. This study demonstrates that experiential methodology in music teaching and learning can be, at least, effective as a lecture approach (Altenmuller, et al. 1999).

But another interesting fact emerged, as well. The two groups showed different brain activation patterns while learning the same material, indicating that the brain had stored it differently. Exhibiting more cerebral cortex activation, the interactive learners when compared to the passive group one year later, still outperformed their counterparts. This suggests that while teachers may be able to achieve equal test score results with lecture formats, when compared over the long haul, active learning offers superior retention.

## ON A PRACTICAL NOTE

Music may help encode memories. Experiment with it in the classroom. Try it as background accompaniment; then try it as a carrier of information. Simple pre- and post-test scores can be administered and effects compared. Ideally, music will be totally integrated into your curriculum, and on equal footing with content.

## RECOMMENDED SELECTIONS

For music with a strong upbeat tempo, try Flamenco music from Spain (Flamenco: Fire and Grace) Cossack music from Russia (Old Believers: Songs of the Nekrasov Cossacks), techno, vocals, and drums from Polynesia (Fenua).

# PART THREE:

# Music in Action

- ◆ LISTENING AND LEARNING
- ◆ GETTING STARTED
- ◆ IMPLEMENTATION NOTES
- ◆ CHOOSING YOUR MUSIC
- ◆ KNOW YOUR MUSIC
- ◆ POLICY IMPLICATIONS

# Listening and Learning

Listening to selected sounds may improve neuromaturation and enhance social skills, language learning, rehabilitation, and relaxation. Music and voice listening requires active participation by the listener. If, in fact, listening skills can be improved through training, the learning implications are, indeed, significant. Let's take a closer look at the evidence that supports this position.

Listening and hearing are very different functions. Hearing is simply the ability to receive auditory information through the ears, bones, and skin, while listening, on the other hand is the delicate ability to *filter*, *analyze*, and *respond* to sounds. In short, listening is an active and refined skill set, while hearing is a passive experience. The impact of this is powerful. What if many learners were hindered not just by poor hearing (as many are), but by poor listening skills? After all, we live in a society in which ambient noise is the norm. Consider that a whopping 25 percent of all Americans have hearing loss and twenty million are regularly exposed to dangerous sound levels (Campbell 1997). From workplace machinery and freeway traffic to blowdryers, music headphones, and rock concerts, we have become a nation bombarded daily by too much noise. Listening is as important as ever, but ever increasingly difficult to do in such a noisy environment.

Fortunately, we can actually train our brains to listen, rather than merely hear. The theory that it is possible to enhance our lives by improving listening skills is based on the work of Dr. Alfred Tomatis, a French ear, nose, and throat specialist. Tomatis pioneered the use of sound stimulation for listening enhancement. He discovered that a listening program consisting of filtered and unfiltered music and voice, received both actively and passively for sixty to seventy-five hours, changed how the subject's brain heard. The Tomatis Method, as it has become known, trains the ear (auditory system in the brain) until the listener can retain the skills without additional training (Tomatis 1991, 1996).

 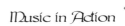

# THE REORGANIZED BRAIN

Tomatis believes that once the ear (hence, our brain) has been trained to listen to music in an active way, as opposed to passively hearing it, a domino effect can take place in which other systems in the human body also potentially reorganize. Tomatis says that sound provides an electrical charge that potentially energizes the brain. He has devised an auditory stimulation process that identifies various dysfunctional physical or motivational systems related to listening, hearing, communicating, and movement, and corrects them via specially filtered classical music, including that of Mozart, as well as selected chants.

Did you know that your own voice range could either bring you down or inspire you? It's been known for some time that cells in the cortex of the brain act like small batteries, which generate the electricity you see in an EEG printout. Tomatis discovered that specific high frequencies actually sped up the brain's recharging process and impacted posture, energy flow, attitude, and muscle tone. The most powerful high frequencies are those in the 8000-hertz range. Tomatis further determined that while the higher frequencies powered up the brain, low

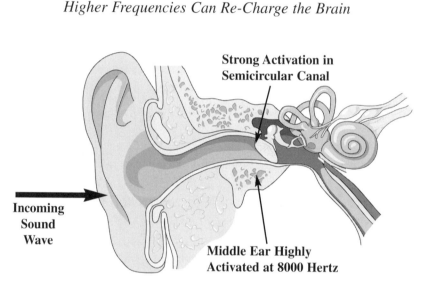

*Higher Frequencies Can Re-Charge the Brain*

**Strong Activation in Semicircular Canal**

**Incoming Sound Wave**

**Middle Ear Highly Activated at 8000 Hertz**

frequency tones discharged mental and physical energy (stress). Tomatis's position is that the ear is a major integrator of the nervous system. Many believe that hyperactive children may be propelled into constant motion because this state "charges up" their brain. We know that movement stimulates the vestibular system, and this theory would help explain the calming effect music can have on hyperactive children. On the other hand, lethargic students can benefit from music's recharging influence on the nervous system, as well.

## LEARNING TO LISTEN

Many students who are having difficulty in school may have listening and/or hearing problems, and these problems may be negatively impacting their behavior, reading abilities, and attentional patterns. Schools ought to test for *both hearing and listening skills*. There are, according to Tomatis, at least seven capabilities of listening, and these can be nurtured at any age:

1. **The ability to select and distinguish tonal differences. This is especially important for reading skills.**

2. **The ability to consciously attend to, and focus on, a certain listening task. This is especially important for following directions, concentration, and short-term memory.**

3. **The ability to process information similarly with both ears. This helps with rhythm and organization.**

4. **The ability to identify the source and direction of sounds. This relates to both reading and following directions.**

5. **The ability to prioritize and tune into higher frequency sounds, while tuning down the lower frequency sounds. This enhances both language and mood control.**

6. **Right ear dominance. This relates to singing on key and academic performance because the right ear sends information to the left hemisphere—the more linear, analytical side of our brain.**

7. **The ability to listen at a healthy normal sound threshold. Some research has correlated hearing loss with lower IQ.**

## ON A PRACTICAL NOTE

Teach students to listen. Quiet the room and ask everyone to listen to the world for a moment. After one minute of silence, let them pick up a pen and write down every sound they heard. Another good listening exercise is to have students listen carefully to an uplifting music selection, while noting subsequently how many different instruments they heard. Give learners the opportunity to compare their notes with each other, and then repeat the exercise. Several weeks later, do the activity again, only this time, have learners compare their prior listening results with the present ones. Are their listening skills improving?

## VOICE THERAPY

If active listening to particular sounds can enhance the brain's systems, as Tomatis believes, there ought to be some practical applications that support this position. Might examples be found in the research on healing? The late Dr. Paul Moses, an eminent professor of speech and voice at Stanford University School of Medicine and an early pioneer in the field, used his listening skills to reveal a Rorschach-like insight into his patients (Campbell 1998). Paul Newham, founder of the International Association for Voice and Movement Therapy in London, has since developed a voice therapy program that is effective. Newham and Campbell both report hundreds of anecdotal cases that support the theory that voice therapy, at the very least, can improve healing and energy, and may even reorganize the brain.

The question then follows, might it also enhance auditory processing for those with phonological deficits? Although, thousands of students a year enroll in courses for this purpose (Gilmore 1982), is there evidence that it works? Some independent researchers have validated that Tomatis's methods do improve stuttering (Badenhorst 1975); and more recently, the research of two neuroscientists, Merzenich and

Tallal, has confirmed that cortical reorganization through altered auditory input can, in fact, improve reading skills (Tallal, et al. 1996). Other benefits that have been noted by researchers and mentioned by parents include the following:

- **Communication**
- **Attention span**
- **Reading comprehension**
- **Quality of speech**
- **Memory**
- **Spelling**

A six-month follow up with the subjects showed that 83 percent of the children maintained or improved upon the gains; 14 percent retained some of the gains; and only 3 percent did not (ibid). This suggests that the process of enhancing the neural system may result in a ripple effect that also aids other systems in the body. The results could not be attributed to a short-term Hawthorne Effect, Arousal Effect, or Attentional Bias Effect. The brain was actually retrained or reorganized in some fashion.

## ON A PRACTICAL NOTE

The music that energizes us normally (but not always) has the following characteristics: (1) A brisk tempo of 75 or more beats per minute; (2) Performed in a major (upbeat) key; (3) Strongly rhythmic (for large muscle energy) or is performed in strings (for inspiration); and (4) A strong personal connection or association with the music is present.

## RECOMMENDED SELECTIONS

For listening as a warm-up to singing, it's tough to beat George Frederick Handel's Hallelujah Chorus. Other fabulous selections include The Sunday Baptist Choir group, An English Ladymass, The Emma Kirby Collection, and Music for St. Anthony of Padua.

# SINGING THERAPY

If listening to one's own voice is therapeutically beneficial, as Tomatis believes, might a singing program enhance academic performance? A high-school choral program involving forty tenth-grade students was studied for possible benefits. The student progress was documented through subject surveys, case studies, interviews, observations, recorded performances, projects, and videotaped interviews. The goal in this course was singing mastery, and 72 percent of the students progressed to the final stage of learning readiness. Also, twenty-six of forty students demonstrated growth in problem solving (Truglio 1990). While additional studies are called for, early evidence indicates that educational benefits may be derived from a singing program.

In Hungary, where math and science scores top the United States by a wide margin, a widely used method of music teaching may be partly responsible for their academic success. Called the Kodaly Method, (derived from the work of Zoltan Kodaly), it involves the teaching and learning of singing in perfect pitch starting with folk songs. Later, students learn to read music and sing pieces composed for an instrument in perfect pitch. This attention to sound seems to pay off. The Kodaly Method has grown worldwide, and students from its ranks exhibit good overall learning scores.

In Harlem, where schools are legendary for high dropout rates, a boys choir may be positively influencing members' decisions to attend college. In spite of the extra time requirements, more than ninety percent of the boys choir participants go on to college! (Gregorian 1997). While some might think that engaging in a high-commitment activity like this would add to a student's workload stress and reduce their study time, results suggest the contrary. Rather, boys choir members seem to have lower stress levels and higher levels of motivation to achieve. While this example certainly doesn't represent a random sample, the results are attention getting.

In a group involving cognitively-delayed two- to five-year-olds, ten weeks of singing and musical activities reportedly increased their vocabulary and language test scores (Hoskins 1988). On the other hand, a study involving developmentally normal three-year-olds receiving twice-weekly singing and music instruction over a three-year period showed no measurable differences in IQ *scores* (weighted towards math and memory) when compared to a control group. Other measures, however, indicated remarkable results (Kalmar 1982), such as improvement in the following areas:

- **Motor development coordination**
- **Abstract conceptual thinking**
- **Play improvisation**
- **Verbal abilities**
- **Creativity**

Dr. Amen, a psychiatrist whose specialty is neurological damage, says that singing is an excellent therapeutic choice for those with mild to moderate temporal-lobe damage (Amen 1997). He also recommends listening to upbeat instrumental music as a tool for behavior change. Symptoms of temporal-lobe damage can include hallucinations, seizures, rage, outbursts, amnesia, panic, confusion, and cult-like affinities. Singing and music seem to activate and stabilize this critical brain area.

## ON A PRACTICAL NOTE

Encourage your students to get involved with school or church choirs or to create their own singing group! Almost any kind of singing is helpful before age twelve, but it is a good idea to wait until after age twelve to begin intensive vocal training. A great song for vocal warm-up is Mozart's Magic Flute. After the warm-up period, traditionals are a great singing choice (i.e., I've Been Working on the Railroad or She'll Be Comin' Around the Mountain, etc.). Hap Palmer songs and Disney soundtracks also provide good sing-along accompaniment.

# Getting Started

## PLAYING MUSIC WITH INSTRUMENTS

It is a good idea to introduce instrumental music instruction early on. Researchers Dr. Rauscher and Dr. Shaw feel strongly that a great benefit of keyboard instruction is the visual-linear representation with a kinesthetic (finger touch) link. The students see the keyboard and spatially link up the touch with the sounds. Remember that while many other instrument lessons may produce significant outcomes (i.e., flute, recorder, guitar, or the Suzuki Method), so far, the only evidence of increased spatial-temporal reasoning comes from keyboarding instruction over a seven-month time frame. To last, the brain changes must be reinforced through continued music training over the long haul.

However, countless music and nonmusic teachers would argue simply for playing any instrument. From tambourines to violins, from percussion to piano, simply having students create music is powerful. Get students involved in the creation, analysis, and enjoyment of music. Use the music as a tool for self-expression, cultural exchange, or simply the pursuit of enjoyment. Get students involved. This seems to be the take-home message we've learned from the research.

## MUSIC AS A CARRIER

Music, when used as a carrier (or accompaniment) to content learning, provides a powerful superhighway straight to the brain. The value of embedding lyrics in music is that learning this way activates emotional responses, as well as memory in the auditory cortex. Songs, specific melodies, rhythms, and tones all have the potential to engage content learning in this way. How, for example, did you learn the alphabet? With a song! Referred to as The A-B-C Song, it is, of course Twinkle, Twinkle Little Star, originally a

Mozart composition. Several repeated actions or hand motions accompanying the song further enhance the learning by providing a reflexive response, which acts as a trigger for the associative cortex. Learning this way is not only more fun, content gets stored in multiple memory pathways making retention and recall more likely.

A common, but highly underutilized "carrier" strategy is to have students replace the existing lyrics of a song with new concepts or words they are learning. As they assemble, arrange, manipulate, and combine words to fit the music, the learning gets reinforced along multiple memory pathways. And working in teams or pairs, of course, increases cooperation, lexical flexibility, and positive emotions as well. Your learners will soon associate music, choreography, and performance with fun, rather than labor.

*Learning content can be "hooked" to music in a variety of ways:*

◆ Use existing music with existing words: Students perform classic musicals like West Side Story.
◆ Create new music with new words: Students create original compositions with drums, keyboards, or other instruments with content they've learned. Rap is one example.
◆ Add new words to existing lyrical music: Take a song like Rock Around the Clock and put new words to it that relate to current learning.
◆ Add words to existing instrumentals: For example, the A-B-C Song or as in a concert-style reading.

# STUDENT-PERFORMED MUSICALS

Conducting student musical performances of classics and standards, as originally written, is also a good use of time. Choose the musical carefully, however, as its lyrics will be heard and performed over and over. At LeMoyne College, 137 undergraduate students volunteered for an experiment. All read lyrics, half of which were happy and half of which were sad. For each of the two conditions, there were three possible musical accompaniment variations: no music, happy music, and sad music. The biggest variation was reported between the music and no music groups. Since the students had no control over the type of music, the no music group had better recall than those with music (Sousou 1997).

This study supports the suggestion that music has the potential to aid in word recall, but not any song will help every student. The key is getting the lyrics embedded in long-term memory. Thus, use lyrics that have a positive message and that resonate emotionally with your learners. Class performances, which take months to plan, design, and rehearse, provide an excellent "stage" for cognitive and emotional development.

# COMPOSING ORIGINAL MUSIC

When students compose their own music set to their own words, they get a chance to experiment with rhythm, timing, beat, melody, and pitch. At the same time, content learning is reinforced through the writing and singing of their lyrics. Like rap, when students create music that is highly personal, they remember it. The creative writing part of this learning allows students to select what's most important, and then to arrange the material into a meaningful theme instead of a dry stream of text. The brain is better able to recall material that is emotionally embedded and presented in story form. If desired, students can use familiar themes (i.e., Goldilocks and the Three Bears, Cinderella, or Peter and the Wolf), then re-write the story with the new content and add a musical background.

Even with very little musical training, learners can play drums and/or keyboards to compose the music accompaniment. Because this project can take as little or as long as you allow, make sure you match the time given with the standards of excellence you expect.

# ADDING NEW WORDS TO EXISTING MUSIC

Adding new words to existing music can be done fairly quickly. Take an existing standard (i.e., Happy Birthday, Jingle Bells, Old MacDonald, Row, Row, Row Your Boat) and rewrite the lyrics incorporating new content. For example, eight-year-olds might create and sing a song like this: "Old Mac Donald had a sun, e-i-e-i-o. And around this sun, nine planets spun, e-i-e-i-o...etc." Older students will want to incorporate contemporary music. However, songs from the 1950s and 1960s are often more suitable due to lyric clarity and brevity. Consider using songs like Rock Around the Clock (Bill Haley and the Comets), Splish Splash (Bobby Darin), Oh, Pretty Woman (Roy Orbison), and Do-Wah-Diddy (Manfred Mann).

Creating student teams for this project is a good idea. Have them first brainstorm some key words or concepts from the content they are learning, then select a song and add new lyrics. Provide them with a song sheet. If you're short on time, have students brainstorm just five words and do only one or two verses. Keeping a box of props available for their staged performance is a good way to keep involvement and fun quotients high. Encourage teams to provide both feedback and applause when the other teams perform.

# SETTING NEW WORDS TO EXISTING INSTRUMENTALS

When writing content-based lyrics for existing instrumentals, use a melody that is highly familiar. For example, The A-B-C Song (which is the same as Twinkle, Twinkle, Little Star), in most cases is known by everyone. The song is already memorized, so the new lyrics will be easier to remember. In fact, it will stick like Velcro!

# CONCERT READINGS

Another useful variation on this strategy is to perform a "concert reading." Concert reading, a technique introduced by the noted Bulgarian educator Dr. Georgi Lozanov, deliberately uses music as a carrier of planned content, creating an effect like a movie soundtrack, play, or opera. The presenter delivers content in accompaniment with dramatic background music. Rather than competing with the music, however, the presenter ebbs and flows with the music. Lozanov discovered that this technique can open gateways to learning, reach the subconscious, create better understanding, activate long-term memory, and reduce overall learning time. It's the difference between watching a movie with or without a soundtrack. Try the mute button the next time you watch a movie and see for yourself. Model the process first; then, ultimately, students can learn to perform concert readings, too.

Music acts as a premium quality signal carrier, whose rhythms, patterns, contrasts, and varying tonalities encode any new information. Use music as a partner. Ride the waves of sound like a "sound surfer," while you ebb and flow with the rhythm. How can music accelerate learning in this way? It activates and elicits emotional responses in the parts of the brain that are also responsible for long-term memory. This means that when information is imbued with music, there's a greater likelihood that the brain will encode it for the long term. The following represent the three stages of a concert reading:

## 1. Preview
Previews are conducted at the beginning of a class when a new topic is introduced. While setting the stage for the day's learning, the preview aspect of a concert reading introduces key ideas set to brief selections of fun, intriguing, attention-getting music. The preview can also be done as a chorus, parable, chant, or poem. The purpose is to build confidence and anticipation. Therefore, keep it brief: Two to four minutes is a good general rule.

## 2. Active Concerts

The purpose of the active concert stage is to deliver content. Present the detailed material as a dramatic presentation using classical or romantic selections (not Baroque). Beethoven, Tchaikovsky, or Haydn can all work. Encourage students to keep their eyes, ears, and minds open. Metaphors can be used to put the new material in context. Some teachers actually create original scripts. Generally this aspect of a concert reading lasts seven to ten minutes. Before speaking, let the music play for ten to thirty seconds to allow learners a moment to feel receptive. Do not compete with the music. Rather "sound surf" with it. This means taking advantage of musical pauses to speak and allowing the music to dominate otherwise. Choosing music, therefore, with appropriate highs and lows is important.

## 3. Passive Review

The passive review is a relaxed, low-key summary of the key points set to Baroque music (use selections in a major key, adagio movements). Students are relaxed, with eyes closed. The passive review usually lasts five to eight minutes and is conducted at the close of a learning session. The emphasis is on relaxation, as this state will allow the brain to better fix content.

## CONCERT READING TIPS

### *Content Familiarity*

Make sure that you are well versed in the content you are teaching. Tell students what you plan to cover. Give them a short verbal preview of the material. Do this even if you are also providing handouts or other visual matter.

### *Music Familiarity*

Make sure that you have listened to your music many times so that you know it inside out. How long does the introductory movement last? When does tempo increase and decrease? When does the volume drop or rise? Decide when it is best for you to speak and when it is best to let the music dominate.

### *Environment*

Create a positive environment. Allow students to sit comfortably. You may wish to adjust the lighting. Have learners stand and stretch, or do some deep breathing warm-ups. Verbalize positive suggestions of expectancy.

## Credibility

When introducing the music, provide the name of the selection, the composer, the period, and any interesting facts you may know about the piece. If learners end up trying to identify this information themselves, they may become distracted.

## Volume

Moderate the volume so that it is high enough to fill in the nonspeaking parts, but low enough so that you can talk when the music ebbs.

## Pause

Get the attention of the audience and create anticipation by pausing at opportune times. Wait to begin reading until the introductory movement is over and the music has ebbed. Usually the prelude lasts from five to thirty-five seconds.

## Dramatic Movements and Voice

Make large movements and gesture dramatically to emphasize key points. Think of yourself as a Shakespearean performer and enjoy making a show. Finish with a dramatic statement or closing remark.

## Experiment and Empower!

Doing concert readings is a great way to have fun, be creative, and embed deep and powerful learning. Repetition is the secret to comfort, and with comfort, you get confidence and competency. Once you have modeled the process for students several times, allow them to conduct their own concert readings. Working in teams reduces "performance pressure" and is a great way to integrate cooperative learning.

# OTHER INTENTS AND PURPOSES FOR MUSIC IN THE CLASSROOM

## Music for Arousal Effect

Arousal represents a change in EEG activity and pulse rate. While helping to engage multiple memory pathways and increasing receptivity, music-induced arousal states (such as calm, curious, expectant, energized, or mystified) are known to enhance and accelerate learning.

## Background Music

Sounds from nature offer a soothing, unobtrusive background accompaniment, which many learners find relaxing and helpful. From waterfall sounds to the ocean or rain forest, the key to effective background music is that it doesn't distract. This is why Baroque is also a good choice for background music: It's very predictable.

## Openings

Get your class off to a good start. From the outset, music can help establish a positive mood, state, tone, and theme for subsequent learning.

## Unity

Music can help break down artificial barriers between individuals. Play selections from various cultures, while learners exchange simple information with each other. Prime students with such questions as, Where was the student who is standing next to you born? What are your goals for the day? What is your favorite subject or hobby? Use the simple law of sound and distance: At twice the distance, sounds have to be four times louder to be heard as loud. Keep music at a moderate volume level, so that students don't have to shout to hear each other.

## Focused Concentration

Music that enhances concentration usually ranges from sixty-five to eighty beats per minute and is played in a major key. It possesses a predictable rhythm and symmetrical form with a consistent volume level and no distracting variances or vocals. Many jazz or Baroque selections meet these criteria.

## Transitions

Music can provide an effective means for mentally shifting gears. If you watch sitcoms, you'll hear the musical interludes that move you mentally from one scene to another. Combine music with stretching and you'll have created the perfect transition activity.

## Punctuate an Activity

While doing an art project, for example, music can strengthen the emotional state of the art theme. Students who are cleaning up materials and supplies will do it much faster to the backdrop of the William Tell Overture. Or, for visualization, use the music of David Kobialka. Play a piano or harp selection while leading students in a stretching break.

## State Management

To evoke curiosity, play the theme song from Peter and the Wolf. To promote creativity, use Sonata for Two Pianos in D Major by Mozart. As a form of celebration, play music that celebrates. To accent a mood of anticipation, play the theme from Jaws or Mission Impossible.

## *Music as a Primer*

Here, we enter the world of Dr. Gordon Shaw and Dr. Frances Rauscher. These two researchers co-discovered the priming element of "The Mozart Effect." While they believe it is the complexity of Mozart that influences the firing patterns in the cerebral cortex to enhance spatial-temporal reasoning, another researcher, Dr. Larry Parsons disagrees. He believes that it's not the complexity but the subelements of Mozart that are influential. Parsons found that rhythms are superior to Mozart in priming spatial-temporal tasks. The point here is not who is right, but the fact that different kinds of music can accomplish different learning goals.

Some of the conditions for effective priming are (1) There must be a target task in mind; (2) The learner must be exposed to a specific piece of music for at least ten minutes; and (3) The target task must be performed within five minutes since the listening effect only lasts thirty minutes or less. If you use a piece of music that makes you feel better, that's arousal. If you hear a piece of music before attempting a task and you perform better subsequently, that's the priming effect. While the effects of priming may be short term, it's worth experimenting with to identify which types of music may have a powerful priming effect for specific activities or disciplines.

For example, rhythms may evoke spatial rotation better than Mozart, but does Gershwin evoke better poetry than Wynton Marsalis? We do not know yet. Widespread educational trials are necessary to find out what kind of music works best for particular learning tasks (and with what population sample).

# WHERE TO GET YOUR MUSIC

◆ Start with what's free! Ask for donations! Students sometimes have CDs they no longer want and are happy to donate or lend.

◆ Buy used music. Most communities have at least one used music shop which offers an economical way to buy used CDs (sometimes at half price or less).

◆ Search the discounted bins in the large chain music stores! Many of the music selections you'll want will be the ones others don't want. Pick up Baroque selections, classical, and folk music at a fraction of the price charged for hot new contemporary selections.

◆ Download music from the Internet. The sound quality is good and if your computer has the memory, it doesn't take long. It's ideal if you have a DSL line. You will need a MP3 device and recordable CDs to record it.

◆ Instead of buying major labels, where you'll only use a third or so of the songs on the CD, customize a CD for your purposes. While the price is a bit higher, the value is well worth it. Why pay $18 to use only three songs when you can pay $18 for a convenient "greatest hits" collection? Visit: www.music maker.com.

◆ Know the copyright laws! If you are an elementary-school teacher playing music in the classroom, a music license is not needed. If, however, you are a staff developer, administrator, secondary- or college-level teacher playing music for public consumption, you do need a license. An annual "blanket license" can be purchased for $100. This allows you to play the music of any artist for cumulative audiences up to 2000 persons a year. A minimal per person fee is enacted after the 2000 maximum is reached. Visit www.bmi.com or www.ascap.com for licensing information.

# Implementation Notes

*T*here are many ways to incorporate the musical arts into the school setting—from lessons involving a particular instrument to marching band participation, from singing in a choral group to passive exposure, from folk dancing to beating drums. Depending on a variety of variables, such as teacher preference, resources available, and the age and experience level of learners, integrating music into the curriculum can take many forms. Whatever form it takes in your classroom or school, keep these tips in mind:

◆ Explain to your students why music is important and what you hope to achieve by exposing them to it. Demonstrate how various types of music impact us differently. Include music that calms, energizes, and inspires. The older your students are, the more they'll appreciate your explanations. Including learners in the decision-making process will help them develop a sense of personal responsibility and intrinsic motivation. Introduce them to emerging theories about music and its impact on the brain and learning. Encourage them to continue their music study at home.

◆ When selecting music to be played or learned in class, you need to be sure that it is appropriate. Although it is good to involve students in the music selection process, don't introduce any selections that you have not previously heard and approved. Incorporating diverse genres, even though they may not be your personal favorites, is fine, but the risk of exposing learners to music with negative, violent, sexist, or racial overtones is too great to take lightly. Be certain that the mood of the music is the mood you want to encourage in the classroom.

◆ Once you've introduced music into the classroom setting, involve students in the management of it. Give them a leadership role. Many are happy to play "disc jockey" for the day, but be sure to reinforce clear ground rules. CD players that allow for multiple discs to be shuffled and mixed are great. If necessary, secure the player to a permanent structure in the classroom with a bicycle lock.

◆ While incorporating the musical arts into your program, conduct classroom experiments. Team up with another teacher at the same grade-level to get a control and experimental group. Or ask another teacher to use one type of music, while you try another, then compare effects. Incorporate pre- and post-tests, note any changes, and survey students on how they believe the music impacted their learning. Involve students in the planning and evaluation phases of the experiments.

◆ Approximately 15 to 25 percent of any audience will be highly sensitive to sounds. These individuals are often musicians or, at least, auditory learners. Remember that not everyone hears music the same way. If students complain about it, ask them for suggestions. Create options so that if learners are distracted, rather than aided, by music, they don't have to listen to it. Explain that the music time is limited and that you respect their learning differences. Remember, no matter what approach you're using at any given time, approximately one-quarter of the class will not prefer it. This is why choice and variety are so important.

◆ If you choose to incorporate background music, keep the volume down to an unintrusive level. Some learners will learn better with background music, and some will be distracted by it. To date, there is no evidence that background music is better all the time; however, the consensus is that it can put some students in a more receptive learning state. Keep these tips in mind when choosing background music: (1) Select it carefully; (2) Make sure it's predictably repetitive; (3) Selections played in a major key are best for productivity; and (4) Instrumentals (with no lyrics or vocals) are less distracting.

◆ Many students who complain about music are doing it because "It's the thing to do." Adolescents especially are in the habit of putting down other people's tastes in everything from relationships to music. This aspect of teen culture is probably best ignored. However, many will complain because of another issue: control. If the room's too cold, and students can access the thermostat, they complain less. If a certain piece of music is not to their taste, and they can influence what's played or the volume, you'll get fewer complaints. When a student complains, be empathic. Turn down the volume, provide them with headphones, or allow them to sit in a quiet corner.

◆ What you say (and believe) about music will be reflected in learner outcomes. A university study illustrates this point quite well. One group was told that music inhibits learning while another was told it enhances learning. Sure enough, the group that expected it to affect their performance positively scored higher than the negative-expectancy group on subsequent tests (covering material studied while listening to music) (Forster and Strack 1998). It's plausible that the expectation of a negative outcome impacted serotonin or cortisol levels, negating possible positive effects.

◆ Music is great; but silence is golden. If used to extremes, saturation can occur and music will lose its effect. Engage music selectively and purposefully. A general rule is to incorporate music no more than 10 to 30 percent of the total learning time, with two exceptions: (1) When music instruction is the primary focus of the class; or (2) When incorporating environmental sounds, like waterfalls, rain forests, or waves breaking on the beach.

---

**WARNING:**
Use music purposely, not randomly. As a guideline, use it only during 10-30% of total instructional time. Too much music is as bad as none at all. Avoid saturation.

---

# Choosing Your Music

C hoosing appropriate music to play at the right times is both a science and an art. The best way to get started is to make a custom cassette or CD with a variety of selections for various circumstances. Once you feel really comfortable with your first compilation, you can start adding more CDs to your collection. While considering which selections to include, ask what is the feeling or state that I want to evoke? Then pay attention to what happens to your body and mind as you listen to the song. Did it facilitate your target state? Pay attention to the beats per minute (BPM): Songs in the forty to fifty BPM range will be more calming, while the faster pace (120-160 BPM) of a pop or hip-hop tune will increase energy.

There are many different ways to categorize mind states. The speed of the electrical activity of the brain, as measured in cycles per second of oscillation, is one. The most common scientific designations, in this case, are beta, alpha, theta, and delta. Brainwave cycles are different than musical beats per minute. In both cases, however, the greater the number of beats, the more alert the state. The term "beats per minute" refers to the creation and transmission of sound out in the environment, while cycles per second refers to internal brain rhythms. Theoretically, brain rhythms can be independent of external sounds, though they are usually correlated. The four basic brain states are described below:

**BETA** brainwaves are the most common type of brain activity recorded in normal conscious states. Beta brainwaves undulate from eighteen to forty cycles per second. Beta means active. You can induce this state with very upbeat music, such as pop, rock, or up tempo instrumentals. Some classical, jazz, and dance selections also certainly qualify.

**ALPHA** brainwaves are commonly recorded when one is quiet and relaxed. Music can induce this state and activate a kind of creative daydreaming. Usually the eyes are closed. Alpha waves are formed in the frequency range of eight to twelve cycles per second. This state is usually induced with a slower beat, such as found in Baroque compositions, Muzak, soft rock, Kitaro, and smooth jazz.

**THETA** brainwaves, observed mainly in the temporal and parietal regions, are often recorded in states of high creativity. These waves are formed at four to seven cycles per second. This state is the twilight zone between sleep and wakefulness. The music that induces, supports, or maintains this state is the very ethereal slow beat compositions like Brian Eno's "Music for Airports," Daniel Kobialka's releases, Philip Glass, harp instrumentals, and other very slow tempo selections.

**DELTA** brainwaves are common to very deep states of sleep with the waves forming every one to three cycles per second. Breathing is deep, while blood pressure, heartbeat, and body temperature drop. This state is unconscious and is the least understood system. At this level, the brain has tuned out music on a conscious level. This is not appropriate for teaching or training, nor are there any specific recommendations for this state.

Remember also to consider personal preference. Music we like or that resonates with us is more likely to impact us on a physical level (Geringer and Madsen 1987). As the teacher, your own state is fundamental to the overall process. Students pick up nonverbal messages continuously and mirror back what you're feeling. If you feel good about the music, learners will likely feel good about it too. Do offer a variety of sounds though.

## Noticing Sensations

With music playing in the background, invite your students to notice any comforting sensations in their body, such as a pleasant heaviness, warmth, calm, steadiness, and so forth.

## Progressive Relaxation

With soothing music playing, ask your students to visualize their feet, ankles, calves, knees, and so on, successively relaxing each area of the body. Slowly move from the feet up, leaving ample time for the student to completely relax each suggested body part.

## Tension Release

This quick total-body-relaxation technique set to music can be used any time you notice that the class is tense. Have learners tense and hold rigid successive body parts for a few seconds at a time, then ultimately "let go" of the tension. As you slowly move through the body parts from head to toe, suggest that students "see" the tension leaving their body.

## Physical Relaxation

High stress (or distress) negatively impacts learning. Music, however, can help induce a state of relaxation that will increase learner
receptivity. Tension blocks information pathways to the brain and
memory much like a kinked hose hinders water flow to your gar-
den.

## Semi-Guided Imagery

Semi-guided imagery exercises open up students to their deeper
selves. With music playing, ask learners to close their eyes as you
begin to describe a peaceful setting. Leave the visualization open,
however, and invite students to let their imagination finish the story. For example, "You meet a wise old
man or woman and for the next two minutes (which is all the time you need) listen to what he/she tells
you...."

## Unguided Imagery

Elaborate on images that spring to mind from listening to the music or remembering the lesson.
Encourage your students to allow their imaginations to take flight stimulated by the images and emotional nuances in the music.

## Image Streaming

Have students describe to some external receptor, be it a learning partner, private journal, or tape
recorder, all the images, thoughts, impressions, feelings, associations, and spontaneous "stuff" going on
in their mind as they listen to a well-chosen selection. The external focus derived from the describing
aspect of this exercise is critical to the process.

# SUMMARY OF MUSIC SUGGESTIONS

**Artistic Expression**

Music has been a powerful inspiration technique for many creative endeavors. Many famous artists traditionally practiced their craft to music. Art teachers often find that music is especially effective in enhancing the creativity and expressiveness of their students. The music must fit the mood you want to create, however. Experiment with various types from classical (Beethoven) or Romantic (Tchaikovsky) to Jazz (Oscar Peterson, Miles Davis, David Sanborn) or New Age (Windham Hill).

**Background**

Play background music such as the following on low volume: Four Seasons, Spring (Vivaldi), Water Music (Handel), Breezin' (George Benson), Brandenberg Concertos (Bach), Eine Kleine Nachtmusik (Mozart), Music for Accelerated Learning (Halpern), Environmental music (Natural Sounds), and Hot Buttered Soul (Issac Hayes).

**Openings**

Establish a positive, upbeat, inviting, and expectant mood right from the start. Be sure, however, that your opening selection is relevant to your audience. Good choices include Guitar Boogie Shuffle (The Virtues), epic movie soundtracks (Superman, E. T., Rocky, Lawrence of Arabia, Born Free, Dr. Zhivago, Oklahoma, etc.), Wild Weekend (The Rebels), and Walk Don't Run (The Ventures).

**Call-back/ Return-to-Room Songs**

Rock Around the Clock (Bill Haley and The Comets), Chantilly Lace (Big Bopper), Splish Splash (Bobby Darin), Pretty Woman (Roy Orbison), Yackety Yak (The Coasters), and Rockin' Robin, Blue Moon, or Jailhouse Rock (Elvis).

**Relaxation**

Piano Music (Eric Satie), Goldberg Variations (Bach), Music for Airports (Brian Eno), Inner Rhythms (Randy Crafton), and all of David Kobialka's and Michael Jones' CDs.

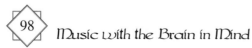

**Brainstorming/ Creative Problem- Solving**

Induce the mind-set for thinking of new ideas, brainstorming, or problem solving with any of the following: Rhapsody in Blue, Piano Concerto in F by Rags Horn Concertos, Clarinet Concerto, Indian Ragas, Concerto for Sitar, Don Juan, Piano Concerto number 5 (Beethoven), Etudes (Chopin), Claire de Lune (DeBussy), Piano Concerto Numbers 26 and 27 (Mozart), Swan Lake Waltz (Tchaikovsky), The Seasons (Haydn), Wake of the Wind (David Arkenstone), Sonata for Two Pianos in D Major: K.448 (Mozart), Theme from Exodus (Handel), Nocturnes (Chopin), Peter and the Wolf (Prokofiev), Egmont Overture (Beethoven), Environmental Music (birds, flute, waterfalls), Passion (Peter Gabriel), Thus Sprake Zarathrustra (2001), Blue Danube (Strauss), Fantasia (Disney), Suites for Orchestra (Bach), Toy Symphonies (Haydn), Musical Joke (Mozart), Desert Vision and Natural States (Lanz and Speer), and Air on the G String (Bach).

**Celebration**

Music can mark a memorable occasion or something positive that you want to remember or want your students to remember. Celebrate the completion of a large class project or anything else with music selections such as the following: Simply the Best (Tina Turner), Celebrate (Three Dog Night), Holiday (Madonna), Hot, Hot, Hot (Chili Pepper), We are the Champions (Queen), Celebration (Kool and the Gang), and Hallelujah Chorus (from Handel's Messiah).

**Spontaneous Playful Responses**

The following musicians tend to evoke a playful state of consciousness, but experiment with their various compositions to determine your personal favorites: Mozart, Haydn, Prokofiev, Ravel, Rimsky-Korsakov, and Seeger. Other good selections include Sleigh Ride, German Dances, The Scarf Dance, Whales and Nightingales, Jonathan Livingston Seagull, Variations on a Nursery Song, The Sorcerer's Apprentice, Lincolnshire Posy, Country Gardens, Story of the Little Tailor, Toy Symphony, March of the Toy Soldiers, John and the Magic Music Man, Sinbad the Sailor, Joseph's Technicolor Dream Coat, Berceuse, Gaite Parisienne, Dance of the Hours, Story of Babar the Elephant, Peter and the Wolf, Tubby the Tuba, Mother Goose Suite, and L'Enfant et les.

**Preschool-Age Children**

Expose young children to a wide variety of music types, including lullabies, world music, jazz, pop, gospel, and dance music. Good composers from the last three centuries include: Bizet, Copland, Delibes, Harsanyi, Haydn, Prokofiev (Peter and the Wolf), Rimsky-Korsakov (Scheherazade), Rossini, Strauss, Villa-Lobos, Weber, and Mendelssohn (Symphony No. 1), Children's Games, Lincoln Portrait, Coppelia, The Story of the Little Tailor, Toy Symphony, Trumpet Concerto, and Overture and Selections from A Midsummer Night's Dream. Other effective titles include Overtures, Blue Danube Waltz, and Little Train of the Caipira.

**Closing Rituals**

Close each day or learning session with a positive song. This ritual can either be done with the same song each day or a different one. Some effective selections include Wonderful World (Louis Armstrong), Happy Days (TV Theme), Happy Trails (Gene Autry), Good Riddance/Time of Your Life (Nimrod), So Long, Farewell (Sound of Music soundtrack), Closing Time (Semisonic), and The Time of My Life (from Dirty Dancing Soundtrack).

**Concert Readings/ Dramatic Storytelling**

Effective suggestions for music accompaniment during a concert reading include: Romeo and Juliet Fantasy Overture (Tchaikovsky), Sonata for One Piano or Second movement, Symphony number 6 (Beethoven), and Music for the Royal Fireworks (Handel). Second movements on classical selections are often slower and more appropriate for concert reading purposes.

**Confidence-Building**

I'll Take You There (Staple Singers), You Can Make It If You Try (Sly and the Family Stone), Take It Easy (Eagles), Be Happy (Bobby McFerrin), I Will Survive (Gloria Gaynor), and Raiders of the Lost Ark Theme (John Williams).

**Creativity**

Good composers and selections for this purpose include Liszt, Respighi, Prokofiev, Rodrigo, Trumpet Concerto, Hungarian Rhapsodies, Ancient Dances and Airs, Pines of Rome, Lt. Kije, Concierto Aranjuez, and Fantasy for a Courtier.

**Dance and Movement for Adults**

Uptempo selections with a strong distinctive beat include YMCA (Village People), La Bamba (Richie Valens), Shout (Isley Brothers), Wear My Hat (Phil Collins), Un-Break My Heart (Toni Braxton), Jellyhead (Crush), Middle-Eastern Belly Dancing, Samba dance tracks, Quad City DJs, Donna Summer CDs, The Best of Chic (Chic), and In the Mood (Glen Miller Orchestra).

**Dance and Movement for Children**

Effective selections include most of the hip-hop artists (those with suitable lyrics); and Brahms, Campbell, Copland, Delibes, Dvorak, Tchaikovsky, Schostakovich, Weber, Hungarian Dances, Lightning on the Moon, Rodeo, Coppelia, Irish Jigs, Slavonic Dances, Dances from Swan Lake, Sleeping Beauty, Polka (from Age of Gold), and Invitation to the Dance.

**Emotional Release**

Suitable composers and selections for this purpose include Chopin, Mahler, Stivell, Strauss, Tchaikovsky, Wagner, Nocturnes, Water Music, Lara's Theme from Dr. Zhivago, Love Theme from Exodus, Symphony Nos. 4 and 6 Verismo Arias, My Own Story, Bravo Pavarotti Scheherazade, Renaissance of the Celtic Harp, Blue Danube, None But the Lonely Heart Prelude, and Love-Death (from Tristan und Isolde).

**Entering a Room with Style**

Try Peter Gunn Theme (Ray Anthony and His Orchestra), Grand March from Aida (Verdi), Tequila (The Champs), Soulful Strut (Young Holt Unlimited), Walk Right In (Rooftop singers), and Let's Get Excited (Pointer Sisters/Patti LaBelle).

**Storytelling**

Try Neverland (Suzanne Ciani), Chrysalis (2002), All Yanni CDs, Summer, Autumn, Spring (George Winston), or Silk Road (Kitaro).

**Focused Concentration**

Try Maiden Voyage (Herbie Hancock), A Change of Heart (David Sanborn), Brandenburg Concertos, Goldberg Variations, 6 Symphonies, Concerto for Two Harpsichords, or The Art of the Fugue (Bach), Symphony Numbers 42, 45, 46, 94, or 100 (Haydn), and Concerti Grossi or Water Music (Handel).

| | |
|---|---|
| *Group Singing/ Chanting* | Day-O, Matilda, or Jump Down Spin Around (Harry Belafonte), Snow White, Songs of the South, Bambi, Dumbo, Winnie the Pooh, Mary Poppins (Disney Soundtracks), Hap Palmer Songs, and Good Morning (Beatles; Sgt. Pepper's Lonely Hearts). |
| *Humor/Ice Breakers* | Try various comedy soundtracks, sound effects, Disney soundtracks (Snow White and the Seven Dwarfs, Bambi, Dumbo, Mary Poppins, and Winnie the Pooh), Gilbert and Sullivan, Toy Symphonies, Irish Jigs, Scottish reels, A Musical Joke, Till Eulenspiegel's Merry Pranks, Musical parodies, Al Yankovich, and Dance of the Sugar Plum Fairy. |
| *Behavior Management* | Incorporate Handel when calling upon cooperative efforts among students. Use Beethoven to promote individual exploration and thinking. Play Bach to help students synthesize multiple information units, different topics, or complex curricula. Play Mozart to get learners to focus their attention on a linear, progressively more complex sequence of operations. And use Haydn to facilitate a child-like delight in and curiosity for new or complex material. |
| *Introductions* | When introducing a student or guest speaker, or when you yourself are being introduced to a class or audience, consider the following music selections to mark the moment: Getting to Know You (from The King and I), Theme from Rocky (Bill Conti), 1984 Summer Olympic Games (John Williams), and Star Wars (John Williams). |
| *Pomp and Circumstance/Fanfare* | Try Fanfare for the Common Man (Aaron Copeland), Triumphal March (Verdi), Persian March, Gypsy Baron, Egyptian March, or Radetzky March (Johann Strauss), Wedding March (Mendelssohn), Rackoczy March from Hungarian Rhapsody (Liszt), and Ninth Choral Symphony (Beethoven). |
| *Special Effects* | To set the stage with feelings of danger, fear, fun, or humor, try Time is Tight (Booker T and the Ms), Jaws theme (John Williams), I'm Walkin' (Fats Domino), Tough New Job (Mission Impossible), Out of Limits (The Markets), Flintstone's Yabba Dabba Doo (Hanna-Barbera's Cartoon Sound FX), Hi-Ho, or Zip-a-dee-do-dah (Disney). |

**Test Preparation/ Study**

Music accompaniment during homework or study time is a highly personal choice: Some prefer it, while others are distracted by it. Auditory processors, for example, tend to prefer silence so they can "hear themselves think." Others find it helps them achieve a relaxed but alert state. Try Baroque, Nature Quest CDs for environmental music, and New Age (Windham Hill).

**Energizers**

Wake up the body and get your learners going with the following selections: Shout (Isley Brothers), Great Balls of Fire (Jerry Lee Lewis), Superstition (Stevie Wonder), Fun, Fun, Fun (Beach Boys), and The Hop (Danny and the Juniors).

**Transition Time/ Mass Movement**

Try the following selections in conjunction with activities, such as cross-laterals, energy-builders, switching seats, etc.: Hawaii 5-0 theme (Ventures), Hurry Up (Road Runner Theme), Hooked on Classics CDs, 1812 Overture (Tchaikovsky), William Tell Overture (Rossini), Theme from Rawhide, Peanuts Theme (Vince Guraldi), and Ride of the Valkyries (Wagner).

**Imagery and Visualization**

Imagery is the ability to create a mental representation of a given scene or series of scenes. Some students report that they cannot create mental pictures. Visualizations and guided imagery are most effective when used in conjunction with the following types of selections: Chariots of Fire and 1492 (Vangelis), all recordings (Kobialka), SeaPeace (Georgia Kelly), Silk Road (Kitaro), Winter, Summer, Fall, Spring (George Winston), and Accelerated Learning (Steven Halpern).

# Know Your Music

### BAROQUE

Composed from 1650 to 1750, baroque is characterized by balance and predictability. It is, therefore, effective for background music. Composers include Albinoni, Bach, Couperin, Handel, Scarlatti, Telemann, Vivaldi, Fasch, and Corelli. Remember that any composition can be slow (largo = 40-60 bpm; larghetto = 60-66 bpm), or medium (adagio = 66-76 bpm; andante = 76-108 bpm), so select your individual movements carefully.

### BIG BAND and SWING

Popularized in the 1940s, big band is a big, brassy sound derived from a larger than average band. Big band and swing music is great for getting people to act, move, or be physical. The tunes are catchy and easy to dance to. Artists include Count Basie, Glen Miller, Les Brown, Benny Goodman, Louis Armstrong, and Fletcher Henderson.

### BLUES

Blues has its roots in the 1800s and continues to be popular today. Originally sung, then written for instruments, the blues have a powerful spiritual and healing effect on many people. Artists include Robert Johnson, Muddy Watters, Fred McDowell, Etta James, Charlie Patton, John Lee Hooker, B. B. King, Sonny Boy Williamson, and Little Walter.

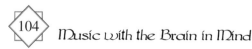

## CHORAL

Choral will forever be associated with George Frederick Handel's Hallelujah Chorus. Other fabulous selections include The Sunday Baptist Choir group, An English Ladymass, The Emma Kirby Collection, and Music for St. Anthony of Padua.

## CLASSICAL

Composed from 1750 to 1820, classical is characterized by variation and expansive creativity with wide ranges. Best for creativity, brainstorming, imagery, and background music. Remember many of the Disney soundtracks are from the classical era with music composed by Beethoven, Mozart, Haydn, DeBussy, Rossini, and Verdi.

## COUNTRY

It started as Western music, but soon found its niche as Country with songs about real people's lives. Artists include Reba MacIntire, Faith Hill, Johnny Cash, Garth Brooks, Shania Twain, and Willie Nelson.

## DIXIELAND

It began as an all-American sound in the late 1800s and reached its zenith in the early 1900s. Countless small up-tempo bands started up with trumpets, drums, percussion, clarinet, and sometimes vocals. Some better-known tunes from this genre include When the Saints, C.C. Rider, Down by the Riverside, Go Down Moses, Go Tell It To the Mountains, and Bugle Call Blues.

## FOLK

Going back centuries, folk has its roots in culture, politics, and oral history. Usually performed with four or less on vocals, very few instruments, and usually one or two acoustic guitars, folk songs reflect a way of life usually transmitted orally from one generation to the next. Many times no surviving record of the original composer exists. American folk artists include Pete Seeger, Woody Guthrie, Peter, Paul and Mary, Bob Dylan, Judy Collins, Arlo Guthrie, and Joan Baez.

## HIP HOP/RAP

The roots of hip hop may go back a long way with only recent recognition of it as its own genre. Artists include Will Smith, L.L. Cool J, Heavy D, and Salt 'n' Pepa. Go to a local music store and ask for recommendations (or ask your students).

## JAZZ

Jazz has its roots in the late 1800s and blossomed in the first few decades of the 1900s with the early greats like Louie Armstrong, Duke Ellington, Roy Eldridge, Dexter Gordon, Dizzy Gillespie, Charlie Parker, Bud Powell, and Miles Davis. Modern jazz is highly diversified with fusionists like Thelonius Monk, Chick Corea, John Coltrane, Cecil Taylor, Buddy Rich, and Harry Pickens. Pop jazz is characterized by artists like Wynton Marsalis, George Benson, and Kenny G. And jazz vocalist greats include Nat King Cole, Billie Holiday, Louie Armstrong, Flora Purim, Chet Baker, Fats Domino, John Coltrane, Ella Fitzgerald, Al Jarreau, and Bobby McFerrin.

## LATINO/TEJANO

With its distinctive sound, latino/tejano emerged during the 1900s. It includes Latin Jazz, Rumba, Salsa, Steel Bands, and Bossa Nova. Tejano, has come into popularity in the last ten years with artists like Selena who have capitalized on the Mexican pop-rock crossover. Go to a local music store and ask for recommendations (or ask your students).

## MOTOWN

Born in Detroit in the 1960s and 1970s, motown was an anthem of sorts celebrating the urban landscape as it developed. It brought the voices of many into popular culture that for too long had not been heard. It is characterized by strong lead vocals with back-up vocals and a strong lead guitar. Artists include Aretha Franklin, The Temptations, The Four Tops, and Stevie Wonder.

## MUSICALS

Both stage musicals and movies evoke deep emotions and milestones in our lives. There's still a lot of gold to be mined from the classics like: Songs of the South (Zip-a-dee-doo-dah), Les Miserables (I Dreamed a Dream), Annie (Tomorrow), Cats (Memory), Chorus Line (One), Man of La Mancha (The Impossible Dream), Funny Girl (People), The Sound of Music (title track), The King and I (Getting to Know You), West Side Story (Maria), and Fiddler on the Roof (If I were a Rich Man).

## POP

Pop has its roots in the early 1900s, beginning with artists like John Phillip Sousa. Its popularity continues today with these well-known artists: Elvis Presley, Sting, The Beatles, Michael Jackson, Carole King, Earth, Wind and Fire, Neil Diamond, Diana Ross, Boyz to Men, Paul Simon, and Anita Baker. Go to a local music store and ask for recommendations (or ask your students).

## RAGTIME

Ragtime started in the late 1800s and flourished after the turn of the century. Great for fun and movement. Artists in this genre include Scott Joplin, Eubie Blake, James Johnson, and Fats Walker.

## REGGAE

Drawn from Afro-American traditions, reggae originated in Jamaica. It eventually flourished in America in the 1960s and 1970s. Among prominent reggae artists are the late Bob Marley, Rita Marley, and Jimmy Cliff.

## ROCK and ROLL

This musical style came into being in the 1950s and its evolution continues at full speed today. Characterized by a lead and bass guitar, with a drummer and two to seven band members, early rockers included Bo Diddley and Chuck Berry. Other popular artists of this genre include The Eagles, The Rolling Stones, The Grateful Dead, Bruce Springsteen, The Beatles, Van Halen, Elvis Costello, Jimmy Buffet, Pearl Jam, U2, Counting Crows, and Aerosmith.

## ROMANTIC-ERA

Romantic-era scores, composed between 1820 and 1870, are characterized by emotional engagement as composers began expressing their responses to literature and other arts through music. The works of the major Romantic composers (i.e., Beethoven, Mahler, and Wagner) form the staple of repertory in modern concert halls and opera houses today. Best for storytelling, evoking emotions, movement, drama, and pomp. Other composers include Tchaikovsky, Strauss, Rimsy-Korssakoff, and Ravel.

## SOUL

Although its roots were established in the early 1900s, soul didn't come into American general consciousness until the 1960s following the rise of rhythm and blues. A strongly emotional type of popular music, soul reflects a "straight from the hip, this is how it is, cut loose, no sugar added, kind of attitude." No attempt to mainstream or doctor it was made. Prominent soul artists include Aretha Franklin, Jackie Wilson, Ray Charles, James Brown, Marvin Gaye, Jackie Wilson, Bobby Womack, Diana Ross, and Wilson Pickett.

## WORLD BEAT

This style gets its unique international sound from ancient and modern cultures. For variation in your classroom, try Flamenco music from Spain (Flamenco: Fire and Grace); Cossack music from Russia (Old Believers: Songs of the Nekrasov Cossacks); klezmer from the traditions of Eastern European Jewry (a big revival movement is occurring); drums from Polynesia (try the group Fenua); Hawaiian instrumentals that include the slack key guitar and ukulele; and African dance music.

# Policy Implications

Our collective wisdom and a host of research studies support the hypothesis that music has strongly positive neurological and system-wide effects. There's no evidence of downside risk; and there's considerable potential for upside gain in both musical and nonmusical outcomes. So far, the evidence suggests that greater benefits are derived from playing music as opposed to listening to it. And, the most significant and lasting effects are derived from long-term music playing. Nevertheless, some effect is still derived from listening (not playing) conditions when compared to nonmusic conditions.

How often should music training occur to maximize the potential of the brain to learn new auditory patterns? Remember the auditory cortex always learns the same way, by repetitive processing of consistent signals. The hippocampus serves as the trainer to the cortex by organizing the new information and presenting it to the cortex. The cortex has a huge memory capacity, but learns slowly. The hippocampus learns quickly, but has a limited storage capacity, so information eventually fades unless it's transferred to long-term memory. This creates a race between the decaying of information in the hippocampus and the time needed for optimal storage in the cortex (McClelland, et al. 1995). As we've all discovered from our own experiences with long information-packed lectures or seminars, we can absorb only so much in one sitting.

To optimize music learning, therefore, it is better to provide frequent short bursts of instruction. The recommended instructional session is sixty to ninety minutes long with a focus on one skill at a time. Longer sessions, up to two hours, can be effective if short concentrated bursts of music training are interspersed with brief periods of alternative activities like dancing, drawing, theater, recess, or walks. Music training is most effective when provided daily, and a minimum expectation should be to provide music instruction at least two times a week. Lasting benefits are best achieved by practicing at least three to six months, and optimal effects are best achieved over a year (at least) of practice and instruction (Weinberger 1998).

Schools that offer a "token" music program, lasting say thirty minutes a week, are missing out on the significant benefits music exposure provides. Some music, however, is still better than none.

Based on the evidence gathered so far, it's both reasonable and prudent to expect that music training should be a basic part of every child's education. Giving children the opportunity to understand and read music, like we teach them to understand and read words, is an ethical, scientific, and cultural imperative. The benefit of starting children early in music training is supported by the research, which suggests that the effects are greater in the early years. In addition, the positive impact of music training increases as children continue to receive instruction.

## STANDARDS FOR TEACHING MUSIC

In the United States, no national music-teaching curriculums or training standards exist. Some children, in fact, never receive the opportunity to even get a modicum of music training. What, if any, music instruction children do receive is usually dependent on the whim of the local district or school, on the contributions of individual classroom teachers, or on what private lessons a child's parents are able to afford. And, this low status position given to music training continues into adulthood.

For comparison, consider that Tokyo maintains ten major professional orchestras, while a major city like San Diego struggles to maintain one. In Japan, a country that mandates music training in school starting at an early age (all children receive a minimum of two music sessions per week), math and science scores soar far above the United State's national average. In Hungary, students receive three classes a week in music unless they enroll in a music magnet school; then they receive it every day. In the Netherlands, music has been a mandatory subject since 1968, and students are assigned comprehensive music/art projects which are required for graduation. The payoff? Math and science scores are near the highest in the world!

These big payoffs come when music education starts early and continues through the years. A last-minute cram course in high school will not produce these kinds of results. The message with music education is, start early, make it mandatory, provide flexible instruction, and support it throughout a student's education. *Music with the Brain in Mind* is an idea whose time has come.

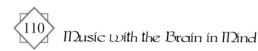

# Appendix

# Glossary

*Adagio* - Music tempo that translates to "at ease." It's a slow movement, characterized by 66 to 76 beats per minute.

*Allegro* - Music tempo that is very brisk—a moderate dance pace. It's best for active situations and is typically characterized by 120 to 168 beats per minute.

*Andante* - Music tempo that is brisk, but not a fast dance pace. It's best for learning situations and is typically characterized by 76 to 108 beats per minute.

*Beat* - The tempo, the pulse, the stable, background pacing of the music. Tap your foot to the music and you'll often find the beat. It ranges most commonly from 50 to 150 beats per minute.

*Harmony* - This is the combination of two or more notes that make a chord.

*Key* - This is the prevailing home base on a piece of music. In most Western music, it's usually the note C. Music can be in a major (slightly more uplifting) key or a minor (slightly more somber) key.

*Largo* - Music tempo that supports relaxation and visualization. It's a slow movement that is characterized by 40 to 60 beats per minute.

*Larghetto* - Slow to moderate music tempo that translates to easy pacing. It's a movement that is characterized by 60 to 66 beats per minute and is useful for learning at a slower pace.

*Major key* - A scale or tones that share compatible overtones and translate to a more harmonious and upbeat mood. The white keys between C and C are the major ones on a piano.

*Melody* - A sequence of tones that often becomes the signature part of a piece of music. It's the "catchy" part of a song that encourages you to want to sing along.

*Minor keys* - This is based on a scale in which the third tone is lowered a half step from the major scale. Beethoven's Fifth goes "tuh-tuh-tuh-dah!" It's often used to create introspection or sadness.

*Pitch* - This is the basic sound wave frequency of a particular instrument. The pitch of a clarinet is different than that of a tuba.

*Presto* - Music tempo that is very fast—an exercise/workout dance pace. It's best for movement only situations and is typically characterized by 168 to 208 beats per minute.

*Rhythm* - This is the pattern the music follows and is determined by the length of sounds or the amount that the sounds are accented.

*Tempo* - This is nothing other than speed of the music. The number of notes jammed into a second turns into beats per minute.

*Timbre* - The identifying acoustic quality of a voice. The timbre of a saxophone is very different than that of a human voice.

# Bibliography

Abikoff, H. 1996. The effects of auditory stimulation on the arithmetic performance of children with ADHD and nondisabled children. *Journal of Learning Disabilities*, May; 29(3): 238-246.

Adaman, Jill and Paul Blaney. 1995. The effects of musical mood induction on creativity. *Journal of Creative Behavior*. 29(2): 95-108.

Alexander, M. and L. Beatty. 1996. Music improves emotional awareness (letter). *Family Medicine*. May; 28(5): 318.

Allen, K. and J. Blascovigh. 1994. Effects of music on cardiovascular reactivity among surgeons. *Journal of American Medical Assocation*. 272: 882-884.

Allen, L.S. and R.A. Gorski. 1991. Sexual dimorphism of the anterior commissure and massa intermedia of the human brain. *Journal of Comnparative Neurology*, 312: 97-104.

Altenmuller, E.; W. Gruhn; D. Parlitz; and J. Kahrs. 1999. Music learning produces changes in brain activation patterns: A longitudinal DC-EEG study. *International Journal of Music Medicine* (in press).

Amen, Daniel. 1997. *Images Into the Mind*. Fairfield, CA: Mindworks Press.

Auditory Processing Problems Linked to Dyslexia. *The Sound Connection*. 1995. Quarterly newsletter of the Society for Auditory Intervention Techniques. 2(3): 4.

Badenhorst. 1975. n'Rorsharchstudie van regssydiges en linksluiteraars met gemengede laterale voorkeure. *Ongepubliseerde M-graad-skripsie*, Pochefstroom, Universiteit vir CHO: Pochefstroom.

Barinaga, M. 1998. Listening in on the brain. *Science*. April 17; 280(5362): 376-378.

Bartlett, D.; D. Kaufman; and R. Smeltekop. 1993. The effects of music listening and perceived sensory experiences on the immune system as measured by interleukin-1 and cortisol. *Journal of Music Therapy*, 30: 194-209.

Bartrop, RW.; L. Lazarus; E. Luckhurst; L.G. Kiloh; and R. Penny. 1977.*Psychosocial Processes and Health: A Reader*. Cambridge, England: Cambridge University Press.

Benson, N. J.; M.W. Lovett; and C.L. Kroeber. 1997. Training and transfer of learning effects in disabled and normal readers: Evidence of specific deficits. *Journal of Experimental Child Psychology*, 64: 343-366.

Berard, Guy. 1993. *Hearing Equals Behavior*. New Canaan, CN: Keats Publsihing.

Bharucha, Jamshed J. 1992. The emergence of auditory and musical cognition from neural nets exposed to environmental constraints. Paper presented at Second International conference on Music Perception and Cognition, UCLA, Los Angeles, CA.

Blood, D.J. and S.J. Ferris. 1993. Effects of background music on anxiety, satisfaction with communication, and productivity. *Psychol. Rep.* Feb; 72(1): 171-77.

Boettcher, W.S.; S.S. Hahn; and G.S. Shaw. 1994. Mathematics and music: A search for insight into higher brain function. *Leonardo Music Journal*, 4: 53-8.

Boltz, M.; M. Schulkind; and S. Kantra. 1991. Effects of background music on the remembering of filmed events. *Memory and Cognition*. 19: 593-606.

Bolwerk, C.A. 1990. Effects of relaxing music on state anxiety in myocardial infarction patients. *Critical Care Nursing Quarterly*. 13(2): 63-72.

Bower, B. 1994. Brain images reveal cerebral side of music. *Science News*, 145(17): 260.

Bouhuys, A.L.; G.M. Bloem; and T.G. Groothuis. 1995. Induction of depressed and elated mood by music influences the perception of facial expressions in healthy students. *Journal of Affective Disorders*. 33: 215-226.

Bronnick, H.; S. Kyllinbgsbaek; I. Law; and O.B. Paulson. 1999. Brain activation during dichotic presentations of consonant-vowel and musical instrument stimuli: a 150-PET study. *Neuropsychologia*. April; 37(4): 431-440.

Brownley, K.A.; R.G. McMurray; and A. C. Hackney. 1995. Effects of music on physiological and affective responses to graded treadmill exercise in trained and untrained runners. *International Journal of Psychophysiology*, 19(3): 193-201.

Bryan, T.; K. Sullivan-Burstein; and S. Mathur. 1998. The influence of affect on social information processing. *Journal of Learning Disabilities*. 31: 418-426.

Butterworth, Brian. 1999. *Hardwired for Math*. New York: Free Press.

Cahill, L; B. Prins; M. Weber; and J. McGaugh. 1994. Adrenergic activation and memory for emotional events. *Nature*. Oct. 20; 371 (6499): 702-4.

Calvin, William. 1996. *The Cerebral Code*. Cambridge, MA: MIT Press.

Campbell, Don. 1998. *The Mozart Effect*. New York: Avon Books.

Catterall, James; Richard Chapleau; and John Iwanaga. 1999. Involvement in the arts and human development: Extending an analysis of general associations and introducing the special cases of intensive involvement in music and theater arts. (in press).

Chan, A.S.; Y.C. Ho; and M.C. Cheung. 1998. Music training improves verbal memory. *Nature*, 396: 128.

Charnetski, Carl and Francis Brennan, Jr. 1998. Effect of music and auditory stimuli on secretory immunoglobulin A (IgA). *Perceptual and Motor Skills*, 87: 1163-1170.

Chase, Marilyn. 1993. Inner music: Imagination may play a role in how the brain learns muscle control. *Wall Street Journal*. (10/31/93) 124: A1.

Chastain, G.; P. S. Seibert; and P. S. Ferraro. 1995. Mood and lexical access of positive, negative and neutral words. *Journal of General Psychology*. 122: 137-157.

Cleall, C. 1983. Notes on a young deaf musican. *The Psychology of Music*. 11: 101-102.

Clynes, Manfred, Ed. 1982a. *Music, Mind, and Brain*. New York: Plenum Press.

Clynes, Manfred, Ed. 1982b. Neurobiologic functions of rhythm, time, and pulse in music. *Music, Mind, and Brain*. New York: Plenum Press.

Cockerton, T.; S. Moore; and D. Norman. 1997. Cognitive test performance and background music. *Perceptual and Motor Skills*, 85: 1435-1438.

Coe, Kathryn. 1990. Art, the replicable unit: Identifying the origin of art in human prehistory. Paper presented at the annual meeting of Human Behavior and Evolution Society, Los Angeles, CA.

Cohen, Nicki S. 1988. The use of superimposed rhythm to decrease the rate of speech in a brain-damaged adolescent. *Journal of Music Therapy*. 25(2): 85-93.

College Board, The: Profile of College-Bound Seniors National Report for 1998, 1999, 2000.

Colwell, C.M. 1994. Theraputic application of music in the whole language kindergarten. *Journal of Music Therapy*. 31: 238-247.

Coulter, D. 1995. Music and the making of the mind: Early childhood connections. *The Journal of Music-and Movement-Based Learning*. 1 (1,2): 22-26.

Creutzfeldt, O. and G. Ojemann. 1989. Neuronal activity in the human lateral temporal lobe: III Activity changes during music. *Experimental Brain Research*. 77: 490-498.

Crick, Francis. 1994. *The Astonishing Hypothesis: The Scientific Search for the Soul*. New York, NY: Charles Scribner & Sons.

Darby, J. and J. Catterall. 1994. The fourth R: The arts and learning. *Teachers College Record*. Winter; 96(2): 299-328.

Demany, L.; B. McKenzie; and E. Vurpillot. 1970. Rhythm perception in early infancy. *Nature*. 226(5604): 718-19.

Diamond, Marian and Janet Hopson. 1998. *Magic Trees of the Mind*. New York: Penguin Group.

Dissayanake, Ellen. 1988. *What Is Art For?* Seattle, WA: University of Washington Press.

Douglas, Sheila and Peter Willatts. 1994. Musical ability enhances reading skills. *Journal of Research in Reading*. 1994, 17: 99-107.

Dowling, W. J. 1993. Procedural and declarative knowlege in music, cognition, and education, in *Psychology and Music: The Understanding of Melody and Rhythm*. Tighe, T. J. and W. J. Dowling (Eds.). Hillsdale, N.J.: Lawrence Erlbaum and Associates.

Edgerton, C.L. 1994. The effect of improvisational music therapy on the communicative behaviors of autistic children. *Journal of Music Therapy*. 1: 31-62

Edwards, E.M. 1974. Music Education for the Deaf. South Waterford, ME: Merriam-Eddy Publishing.

Eisner, Elliot. 1998. Does Experience in the arts boost academic achievement? *Journal of Art and Design Education*. Sept-Oct; 17(1): 7-15.

Elbert, T.; C. Pantev; C. Weinbruch; B. Rockstroh; and E. Taub. 1995. Increased auditory cortical representation of the left hand in string players. *Science*. 270: 305-307.

Epstein, L; M. Hersen; and D. Hemphill. 1974. Music feedback in the treatment of tension headache: An experimental case study. *Journal of Behavior Therapy and Experimental Psychology*. 5: 59-63.

Escher, J. and D. Evequoz. 1999. Music and heart rate variability: Study of the effect of music on heart rate variability in healthy adolescents. *Schweiz Rundsch Med. Prax*. May 20; 88(21): 951-952.

Escher, J.; U. Hohmann; L. Anthenien; E. Dayer; C. Bosshard; and R. C. Gaillard. 1993. Music during gastrocopy (German) Schweitz. *Med. Wochenschrift*. 123: 1354-1358.

Farrell, Michael. 1973. Music and self-esteem: Disadvantaged problem boys in an all-black elementary school. *Journal of Research in Music Education*. Spring; 21(1): 80-84.

Forster, J. and F. Strack. 1998. Subjective theories about encoding may influence judgemental regulation in human memory. *Social Cognition*. 16: 78-92.

Fries, P. 1997. Synchronization of oscillatory responses in visual cortex correlates with perceptin in interocular rivalry. Proceedings of the National Academy of Sciences. 94, 12699.

Furman, C. 1978. The effect of musical stimulation on the brainwave production in children. *Journal of Music Therapy*. 15: 108-17.

Gardner, Howard. 1983. *Frames of Mind*. New York: Basic Books.

Gardstrom, S.C. 1999. Music exposure and criminal behavior: Perceptions of juvenile offenders. *Journal of Music Therapy*. 36(3): 207-221.

Garreau, B. 1994. Evidence of Abnormal Processing of Auditory Stimulation Observed in Cerebral Blood Flow Studies. *Developmental Brain Dysfunction*. 7: 119-128.

Geringer, J. and C. Madsen. 1987. Tuning preferences in recorded popular music. in *Applications of Research in Music Behavior*. Madsen, Clifford K. and Carol A. Prickett (Eds.) Tuscaloosa and London. The University of Alabama Press.

Gerra, G.; A. Zaimovic; D. Franchini; M. Pallidino; G. Giucastro; N. Reali; D. Maestri; R. Caccavari; R. Delsignore; and F. Brambilla. 1998. Neuroendrocrine responses of healthy volunteers to 'techno-music': Relationships with personality traits and emotional state. *International Journal of Psychophysiology*. Jan; 28(1): 99-111.

Gershon, Michael. 1998. *The Second Brain*. New York: Harper Collins.

Gilmore, T.M. 1982. *Results of a Survey of Children's Performance On A Variety of Psychological Tests Before and After Completing the Tomatis Program*. Rexale, Ontario: MDS Health Group Ltd.

Glausuisz, J. 1997. The neural orchestra. *Discover Magazine*. 18(9): 28.

Godeli, M.R.; P.R. Santana; V.H. Souza; and G.P. Marquetti. 1996. Influence of background music on preschooler's behavior: A naturalisitc approach. *Perceptual and Motor Skills*, 82: 1123-1129.

Goleman, Daniel. 1995. *Emotional Intelligence*. New York: Bantam Books.

Graziano, Amy; Matthew Peterson; and Gordon Shaw. 1999. Enhanced learning of proportional math through music training and spatial-temporal training. *Neurological Research*. March; 21(2).

Gregorian, V. 1997. Ten things you can do to make our schools better. *Parade Magazine*, March 23: 6-7.

Gresh, R. 1990. Heightening Aesthetic Response Through the Development and Production of Student-Created Videos. New York: NYU National Arts Education Research Center.

Gunsberg, A. 1991. Play as improvisation: The benefits of music for developmentally-delayed young chidren's social play. *Early Child Development and Care*. 66: 85-91.

Hall, J. 1952. The effect of background music on the reading comprehension of 278 eighth and ninth graders. *Journal of Educational Research*. February; 45: 451-458.

Hodges, D. 1996. *Handbook of Music Psychology*. San Antonio, TX: IMR Press.

Hood, J.D. 1977. Deafness and Music appreciation. in *Music and the Brain*; Critchley, M. and R.A. Henson (Eds.) Springfield IL: Chas. Thomas Publsihing.

Hose, B.; G. Langner; and H. Scheich. 1987. Topographic representation of periodicities in the forebrain of a mynah bird: One map for pitch and rhythm? *Brain Research*. 422: 367-373.

Hoskins, C. 1988. Use of music to increase verbal response and improve expressive language abilities of preschool language delayed children. *Journal of Music Therapy*. 25: 73-84.

Hughes, J.R.; Y. Daaboul; J. J. Fino; and G. Shaw. 1998. The "Mozart effect" in epileptiform activity. *Clinical Electroencephalography*, 29: 109-119.

Hume, K.M. and J. Crossman. 1992. Musical reinforcement of practice behaviors among competetive swimmers. *Journal of Applied Behavior Analysis*. 25(2): 665-670.

Hurwitz, I; P.H. Wolff; B.D. Bortnick; and K. Kokas. 1975. Nonmusical effects of the Kodaly music curriculum in primary grade children. *Journal of Learning Disabilities*. 8: 45-51.

Ishii, C.; S. Hagihara; and R. Minimisawa. 1993. Effects of music on releiving pain associated with compulsory posture. *Nihon Kango Kagakkai* (Journal of Japan Academy of Nursing Science) 13(1): 20-27.

Jensen, R. 1999. *The Dream Society: How the Coming Shift from Information to Imagination Will Transform Your Business*. New York: McGraw-Hill.

Johnson, Julene K; Hellmuth Petsche; Peter Richter; and Astrid Von Stein. 1996. The dependence of coherence estimates of spontaneous EEG on gender and music training. *Music Perception*. 13: 563-82.

Jourdain, R. 1997. *Music, Ecstacy, and the Brain*. New York: William Morrow and Co.

Kalmar, M. 1982. The effects of music education based on Kodaly's directives in nursery school children: From a psychologists's point of view. *Psychological Music*.    Special Issue: 63-68.

Kandel, E.; J. Schwartz; and T. Jessell. 1991. (3rd. ed) *Principles of Neural Science*. Norwalk, CT: Appleton and Lange Publishers.

Klinke, R.; A. Kral; S. Heid; J. Tillein; and R. Hartmann. 1999. Recruitment of the auditory cortex in congentially-deaf cats by long-term cochlear electrostimulation. *Science*. Sept; 10: 285(5434): 1729-33.

Konishi, M. 1994. Pattern generation in birdsong. *Current Opinions in Neurobiology*. 4: 827-31.

Kratus, J. 1989. A Time analysis of the compositional processes used by children ages 7 to 11. *Journal of Research in Music Education*. 37: 5-20.

Kratus, J. 1994. Relationships among children's audiation and their compositional processes and products. *Journal of Research in Music Education*. 42: 115-130.

Krumhans, C.L. and P.W. Jusczyk. 1990. Infants' perception of phrase structure in music. *Psychological Science*. 1: 70-73.

Kumar, A.M.; F. Tims; D.G. Cruess; M. J. Mintzer; G. Ironson; D. Loewenstein; R. Cattan; J. B. Fernandez; C. Eisdorfer; and M. Kumar. 1999. *Alternative Therapy Health Medicine*. Nov; 5(6): 49-57.

Lamb, S.J. and A.H. Gregory. 1993. The relationship between music and reading in beginning readers. *Educational Psychology*. 13: 19-26.

Lane, D. 1992. The effect of a single music therapy session on hospitalized children as measured by salivary immunoglobulin A. (measuring speech pause time and using Patient Opinion Likert Scale). Dissertation Abstracts International, 52(7-B), 3522.

Leader, L.R.; P. Baillie; B. Martin, et al. 1982. The assessment and significance of habituation to repeated stimulus by the human fetus. *Early Human Development*. 7: 211-219.

Lecanuet, J.P.; C. Granier-Deferre; and M.C. Busnel. 1988. Fetal cardiac and motor responses to octave-band noises as a function of cerebral frequency, intensity, and heart-rate variabtility. *Early Human Development*. 18: 81-93.

Malyarenko T.N; G.A. Kuraev; Yu E. Malyarenko; and M.V. Khatova. 1996. The development of brain electric activity in 4-year-old children by long term stimula-    tion with music. *Human Physiology*. 22: 76-81.

Matteis, M.; M. Silvestrini; E. Troisi; L. M. Cupini; and C. Caltigirone. 1997. Transcranial doppler assessment of cerebral blood flow during perception and recognition of melodies. *Journal of the Neurological Sciences*. 149: 57-61.

Mazziotta, J.; M. Phelps; R. Carson; D. Kuhl. 1982. Tomographic mapping of human cerebral metabolism: Auditory stimulation. *Neurology*. 132: 921-37.

McClelland, D.; C. Alexander; and E. Marks. 1980. The need for power, stress, immune function, and illness among male prisoners. *Journal of Abnormal Psychology*. 10: 93-102.

McClelland, J.L.; B.L. McNaughton; and R.C. O'Reilly. 1995. Why there are complementary learning systems in the hippocampus and neocortex: Insights from the    success and failures of connectionist models of learning and memory. *Psychological Review*. 102: 419-457.

McCraty, R.; M. Atkinson; G. Rein; and A.D. Watkins. 1996. Music enhances the effect of positive emotional state on salivary IgA. *Stress Medicine*. 12: 67-75.

McFarland, R.A. and R.F. Kennison. 1998. Asymmetrical effects of music on spatial-sequential learning. *Journal of General Pscyhology*. 115: 263-272.

McKinnery, Cathy and Frederick Tims. 1995. Differential effects of selected classical music on the imagery of high versus low imagers: Two studies. *Journal of Music Therapy*. 22(1): 22-45.

Mikela, Tony. 1990. "Does Music have an impact on the development of students?" A talk prepared for the 1990 state convention of California Music Educators Assn.

Miluk-Kolasa, B.; S. Obminski; R. Stupnicki; and L. Golec. 1994. Effects of music treatment on salivary cortisol in patients exposed to pre-surgical stress. *Experimental and Clinical Endocrinology*. 102(2):118-20.

Mockel, M.; L. Rocker; T. Stork; J. Vollert; O. Danne; H. Eichstadt; R. Muller; and H. Hochrein. 1994. Immediate physiological responses aof healthy volunteers    to different types of music: Cardiovascular, hormonal, and mental changes. *European Journal of Applied Physiology*, 68: 451-459.

Monaghan, P. (1998) Does practice shape the brain? Scientific Correspondence in *Nature*. 394: 434.

Morton, L.L.; M.C. Pietrangelo; and S. Belleperche. 1998. Using Music to Enhance Competence. *Canadian Music Educator*. Summer; 39(4): 13-16.

Muftuler, L.T.; M. Bodner; G.L. Shaw; and O. Nalcioglu. 1999. fMRI of Mozart effect using auditory stimuli. Abstract presented at 7th meeting of International Society for Magnetic Resonance in Medicine, Philadelphia, PA.

National Center for Education Statistics (NCFES). 1998. Mini-Digest of Education Statistics. Wash. D.C. Pgs. 34-35.

Newcomer, J.W.; G. Selke; A.K. Melson; T. Hershey; S. Craft; K.  Richards; and A.L. Alderson. 1999. Decreased memory performance in healthy humans induced by stress-level cortisol treatment. *Archives of General Pscychiatry*. June; 56(6): 527-533.

Noettcher, W.; S. Hahn; and G. Shaw. 1994. Mathematics and music: A search for insight into higher brain function. *Leonardo Music Journal*. 4: 53-58.

Obler, Loraine and Deborah Fein. 1988. *The Exceptional Brain*. New York: The Guilford Press.

Olsho, L.W. 1984. Infant frequency discrimination. *Infant Behavior and Development*. 7: 27-35.

Oppenheimer, T. 1999. Schooling the imagination. *Atlantic Monthly*. September; 284(3): 71-83.

Orsmond, G.I. and L.K. Miller. 1999. Cognitive, musical, and environmental correlats of early music instruction. *Psychology of Muisc*. 27: 18-37.

Overy, K. 1998. Study mentioned in: "Discussion Note: Can music really improve the mind?" *Psychology of Music*. 26: 97-99.

Palmer, Caroline. 1997. Music Performance. *Annual Review of Psychology*. 48: 115-138.

Pantev, C.; Robert Oostenveld; Almut Engelien; Bernard Ross; Larry Roberts; and Manifred Hoke. 1998. Increased cortical representation in musicians. *Scientific Correspondence in Nature*. 396(128): 811-813.

Parsons, L.M.; M.J. Martinez; E.D. Delosh; A. Halpern; and M.H. Thaut. In Process. *Musical and Visual Priming of Visualization and Mental Rotation*.

Pearce, Katy. 1981. Effects of different types of music on physical strength. *Perceptual and Motor Skills*. 53, 2: 351-352.

Peretz, I. and J. Morais. 1993. Specificity for Music. in *Handbook of Neuropsychology*. Boller, F. and J. Grafman (Eds.) Amsterdam: Elsevier Science Publishers.

Persellin, D. 1993. Effects of learning modalities on melodic and rhythmic retention on vocal pitch-matching by preschool children. *Perceptual and Motor Skills.* June; 78 (3, Part 2): 1231-1234.

Pert, Candace. 1997. *Molecules of Emotion.* New York: Scribner and Sons.

Petsche, H. 1993. Brain coherence during music activities. *Music Perception.* 11: 117-151.

Pinker, S. 1997. *How the Mind Works.* New York: WW Norton and Company.

Pratt, Rosalie; Abel Hans-Henning; and Jon Skidmore. 1995. The effects of neurofeedback training with background music on EEG pattersn of ADD and ADHD children. *International Journal of Arts Medicine.* 4: 24-31.

Prokhorov, V. 1998. Will piano lessons make my child smarter? *Parade Magazine.* June 14; pgs. 14-17.

Ramos, J. and M. Corsi-Cabrera. 1989. Does Brain electrical activity react to music? *International Journal of Neuroscience.* Aug; 47(3-4): 351-357.

Rauscher, F.; D. Robinson; and J. Jason. 1998. Improved maze learning through early music exposure in rats. *Neurological Research.* July; 20: 427-432.

Rauscher, F. and G. Shaw. 1998. Key componenets of the Mozart effect. *Perception and Motor Skills.* 86: 835-841

Rauscher, F.; G. Shaw; and K. Ky. 1995. Listening to Mozart enhances spatial-temporal reasoning: towards a neurophysiological basis. *Neuroscience Letters.* 185: 44-47.

Rauscher, F.; G. Shaw; and K. Ky. 1993. Music and Spatial Task Performance. *Nature.* 365: 611.

Rauscher, F.; G. Shaw; L. Levine; E. Wright; W. Dennis; and R. Newcomb. 1997. Music training causes long-term development of preschool children's spatial-temporal reasoning. *Neurological Research.* 19: 2-8.

Reeves, L. and R.W. Weisberg. 1994. The role of content and abstract information in analogical transfer. *Pscyhological Bulletin.* 115: 381-400.

Rein, G. and R.M. McCraty. 1995. Effects of positive and negative emotions on salivary IgA. *Journal of Advances in Medicine.* 8: 87-105.

Richman, B. 1993. On the evolution of speech: Singing as the middle term. *Current Anthropology.* 34: 721-22.

Rider, M. and C. Weldin. 1990. Imagery, improvisation, and immunity. *Arts in Psychotherapy.* 17; 211-216.

Rider, M. and J. Achterberg. 1989. Effects of music-assisted imagery on neutrophils and lymphocytes. *Biofeedback and Self-Regulation.* 14: 247-257.

Riehle, A.; S. Grun; M. Diesmann; and Ad Aertsen. 1997. Spike syncronization and rate modulation differentially involved in motor cortical function. *Science.* 278: 1950.

Rogers, Sally. 1990. "Theories of Child Development and Musical Ability." in *Music and Child Development* . Wilson, Frank B. and L. Franz Roehmann (Eds.) St. Louis, MO: MMB Music.

Sacks, Oliver. 1991. Music , health and well-being. *Journal of the American Medical Association.* 26: 32.

Samson, S. and R.J. Zatorre. 1994. Contribution of the right temporal lobe to musical timbre discrimination. *Neuropsychologia.* 32: 231-240.

Sapolsky, Robert 1992. *Stress, the Aging Brain, and Mechanisms of Neuron Death.* Cambridge, MA: MIT Press; Bradford Book.

Sarntheim, J.; H. Petsche; P. Rappelsberger; G. Shaw; and A. von Stein. 1998. Synchronization between prefrontal and posterior association cortex during human working memory. Proceedings of the National Academy of Sciences. USA; 95: 7092-7096.

Sarntheim, J., A. von Stein; P. Rappelsberger; H. Petsche; F. Rauscher; and G. Shaw. 1997. Persistent patterns of brain activity: An EEG coherence study of the positive effect of music on spatial-temporal reasoning. *Neurological Research.* 19: 107-111.

Scheel, K.R. and J.S. Westefeld. 1999. Heavy metal music and adolescent suicidality: An empirical investigation. *Adolescent.* Summer; 34(134): 253-273.

Schellenberg, E.G. and S.E. Trehub. 1996. Natural musical intervals: Evidence from infant listeners. *Psychological Science.* 7: 272-277.

Schlaug, G.; L. Jancke; Y. Huang; J.F. Staiger; and H. Steinmetz. 1995b Increased corpus callosum size in musicians. *Neurophysiology.* 33:1047-1055.

Schlaug, G.; L. Jancke; and H. Pratt, H. 1995a. In vivo evidence of structural brain assymetry in musicians. *Science.* 267: 699-701.

Schlaug, G.; L. H. Lee; V. Thangaraj; R.R. Edelman; and S. Warach. 1998. Macrostructural adaption of the cerebellum in musicians, *Society of Neuroscience Abstracts.* 24: 2118.

Serafine, M. 1988. Music as Cognition: The development of thought in sound, New York: Columbia University Press.

Sergent, J.; E. Zuck; S. Terriah; and B. MacDonald. 1992. Distributed neural network underlying musical sight-reading and keyboard performances. *Science.* 257(5066): 106-9.

Shaw, G.L; A.B. Graziano; M. Peterson. 1999. Enhanced learning of proportional math through music training and spatial-temporal training. *Neurological Research.* 21(2): 139-52.

Shaw, G.L. 2000. *Keeping Mozart in Mind.* San Diego, CA: Academic Press.

Shaw, G.L. 1978. Space-time correlations of neuronal firing related to memeory storage capacity. *Brain Research Bulletin.* 3: 107-113.

Shaw, G.L.; J. Kruger; D.J. Silverman; A.M. Aertsen; F. Aiple; and H.C. Liu. 1993. Rhythmic and patterned firing in visual cortex. *Neurological Research.* 15: 46-50.

Shaw, G.L.; P.C. Rinaldi; and J.C. Pearson. 1983. Processing capability of the primary visual cortex and possible physiological basis for an apparent motion illusion. *Experimental Neurology.* 79: 293-298.

Shaw, G.L.; M. Sardesai; C. Figge; M. Bodner; J.A. Quillfeldt; S. Landau; and A. Ostling. 1998. Reliable short-term memory in the trion model: Toward a cortical language and grammar. 21st Annual Meeting of the Society of Neuroscience, Abstract 71.9, Los Angeles, CA.

Shaw, G.L.; D.J. Silverman; and J.C. Pearson. 1998. Trion model of cortical organization and the search for the code of short-term memory and information processing. in *Systems with Learning and Memory Abilities.* Levy, J. and J.C.S. Delacour (Eds.) New York, Amsterdam, North Holland.

Shutter-Dyson, R. and C. Gabriel. 1981. (2nd ed.) *The Psychology of Musical Ability.* London: Methuen Books.

Simonds, Roderick and Arnold Scheibel. 1989. The Postnatal development of the motor speech area: A preliminary study. *Brain and Language.* 37: 42-58.

Sousou, S.D. 1997. Effects of melody and lyric on mood and memory. *Perceptual Motor Skills.* Aug; 85(1) 31-40.

Steele, K.M.; J.D. Brown; and J.A. Stoecker. 1999. Failure to confirm the Rauscher and Shaw description of recovery of Mozart effect. *Perceptual Motor Skills.* June; 88(3 pt. 1): 843-848.

Stein, Barbara; C.A. Hardy; and Herman Totten. 1984. The use of music and imagery to enhance and accelerate information retention. *Journal of the Society for Accelerative Learning and Teaching.* 7(4).

Stopfer, M. 1997. Impaired odor discrimination on desynchronization of odor-encoding neural ensemblies. *Nature.* 390: 70.

Stratton, V.N. and A.H. Zalanowski. 1995. The effects of music and paintings on mood. *Journal of Music Therapy.* 26: 30-41.

Stryker, M. 1998. Detroit Symphony Orchestra's visit underscores the importance that Japanese schools place on music education and appreciation. *Detroit Free Press*. Nov 19; 1A.

Stutt, H.A. 1983. The Tomatis Method: A Review of Current Research. Montreal: McGill Univeristy.

Sutter, M.L. and C.E. Schreiner. 1991. Physiology and topography of neurons with multipeaked tuning curves in cat primary auditory cortex. *Journal of Neurophysiology*. 65: 1207-1226.

Swartz D.W. and R.W. Tomlinson. 1990. Spectral response patterns of auditory cortex neurons to harmonic complex tones in alert monkeys. *Journal Neurophysiology*. 64(1): 282-298.

Tallal, P.; S.L. Miller; G. Bedi; G. Byma; X. Wang; S.S. Nagarajan; C. Schreiner; W.M. Jenkins; and M.M. Merzenich. 1996. Language comprehension in language-learning impaired children improved with acoustically modified speech. *Science*. 271: 81-84.

Taniguchi, T. 1991. Mood congruent effects by music on word recognition (Japanese Language) *Shinrigaku Kenkyu*. 62: 88-95.

Terwogt, M.M. and F. VanGrinsven. 1988. Recognition of emotions in music by children and adults. *Perceptual and Motor Skills*. 67: 697-698.

Thaut, Micahel; Sandra Schleiffers; and William Davis. 1991. Analysis of EMG activity in biceps and triceps muscle in an upper extremity gross motor task under the influence of auditory rhythm. *Journal of Music Therapy*. 28: 64-68.

Thayer, Robert. 1996. *The Origin of Everyday Moods*. New York: Oxford Univeristy Press.

Thorpe, L.A. and S.E. Trehub. 1989. Duration illusion and auditory grouping in infancy. *Developmental Psychology*. 25: 122-127.

Tomatis, Alfred. 1996. *The Ear and Language*. Norval, Ontario: Mouling Publishing.

Tomatis, Alfred. 1991. *The Conscious Ear*. Barrytown, NY: Station Hill Press.

Took, K.J., and D. Weiss. 1994. Heavy metal, rap, and adolescent behavior. *Adolescence*. 29: 613-621.

Trehub, S.E.; D. Bull; and L.A. Thorpe. 1984. Infant's perception of melodies: The role of melodic contour. *Child Development*. 55: 821-830.

Trehub, S.E. and L.A. Thorpe. 1989. Infant's perception of rhythm: Categorization of auditory sequences by temporal structure. *Canadian Journal of Psychology*. 43: 217-229.

Truglio, A. 1990. An individualized learner-centered approach for a high school choral program. New York: NYU National Arts Education Research Center.

Upitas, R. 1995. Fostering children's compositions: Activities for the classroom. *General Music Today*. Spring: 16-19.

—— 1992. *Can I Play You My Song? The Compositions and Invented Notations of Children*. Portsmouth, NH: Heineman.

VanderArk, Sherman and Daniel Ely. 1993. Cortisol, biochemical, and galvanic skin responses to music stimuli of different preference values by college students in biology and music. *Perceptual and Motor Skills*. 77: 227-234.

VanderArk, Sherman and Daniel Ely. 1992. Biochemical and galvanic skin responses to music stimuli by college students in biology and music. *Perceptual and Motor Skills*. 74: 1079-90.

Vittitow, M.; I.M. Windmill; J.W. Yates; and D.R. Cunningham. 1994. Effect of simultaneous exercise and noise exposure (music) on hearing. *Journal of the American Academy of Audiology*. Sept. 5(5): 343-8.

Vollmer-Haase, J.; K. Finke; W. Hartje; and M. Bulla-Hellwig. 1998. Hemispheric dominance in the processing of J. S. Bach fugues: A transcranial Doppler sonography (TCD) study with musicians. *Neuropsychologia*, 36: 857-867.

Wallin, N.; B. Merker; and S. Brown. 1999. *The Origins of Music*. Cambridge, MA: MIT Press; A Bradford Book.

Weinberger, N. 1998. Creating creativity with music. *Musica Research Notes*. Vol V(2): 2.

Weinberger, N. and T.M. McKenna. 1987. Sensitivity of single neurons in auditory cortex to contour: Toward a neurophysiology of music perception. *Music Perception*. 5: 355-390

Wigram, Tony and Jos DeBacker (Eds) 1999. *The Clinical Applications of Music Therapy in Developmental Disability, Pediatrics, and Neurology*. London: Jessica Kingsley Publisher.

Wilson, Frank. 1998. *The Hand*. New York, NY: Pantheon Books.

Wingert, M. 1972. Effects of a music enrichment program in the education of the mentally retarded. *Journal of Music Therapy*. 9 (1): 13-22.

Winter, M.J.; S. Paskin; and T. Baker. 1994. Music reduces stress and anxiety of patients in the surgical holding area. *Journal of Post Anesthesia Nursing*. 9: 340-343.

Wolff, K.L. 1979. The effects of general music education on the academic achievement, perceptual-motor development, creative thinking, and school attendance of first graders. Doctoral dissertation, Univ. of Michigan. Diss. Abstracts, 40: 5359A.

Zatorre, Robert J. 1988. Pitch perception of complex tones and human temporal lobe function. *Journal of the Acoustical Society of America*. 84: 566-572.

Zatorre, Robert; Alan Evans; and Ernest Meyer. 1994. Neural mechanisms underlying melodic perception and memory for pitch. *Journal of Neuroscience*. 14(4): 1908-1919.

Zatorre, R.J. and S. Samson. 1991. Pitch processing in brain-damaged patients. *Brain*. 114: 2403-2417.

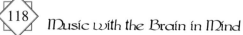

# Other Related Readings From Corwin Press

*10 Best Teaching Practices , 2nd Ed.* (2005) by Donna Walker Tileston

*12 Brain/Mind Learning Principles in Action* (2005) by Renate Nummela Caine, Geoffrey Caine, Carol McClintic, and Karl Klimek

*Building the Reading Brain, PreK-3* (2004) by Patricia Wolfe and Pamela Nevills

*Classroom Activators: 64 Novel Ways to Energize Learners* (2004) by Jerry Evanski

*Designing Brain-Compatible Learning, 3rd Ed.* (2003) by Gayle Gregory and Terrence Parry

*Differentiated Instructional Strategies* (2002) by Gayle H. Gregory and Carolyn Chapman

*Differentiated Instructional Strategies in Practice* (2003) by Gayle H. Gregory

*Differentiating Instruction to Meet the Needs of All Students* (2002) by Carolyn Chapman

*Differentiating Instruction With Style* (2005) by Gayle H. Gregory

*Eight Ways of Knowing: Teaching for Multiple Intelligences, 3rd Ed.* (1998) by David Lazear

*Eight Ways of Teaching: The Artistry of Teaching With Multiple Intelligences, 4th Ed.* (2003) by David Lazear

*Environments for Learning* (2003) by Eric Jensen

*How the Brain Learns to Read* (2005) by David A. Sousa

*How the Brain Learns, 3rd Ed.* (2006) by David A. Sousa

*How the Gifted Brain Learns* (2003) by David A. Sousa

*How the Special Needs Brain Learns, 2nd Ed.* (2006) by David A. Sousa

*How to Explain a Brain* (2005) by Robert Sylvester

*Introduction to Brain-Compatible Learning* (1998) by Eric Jensen

*Learning Smarter* (2001) by Eric Jensen and Michael Dabney

*Learning with the Body in Mind* (2000) by Eric Jensen

*Mindful Learning* (2003) by Linda Campbell

*Music With the Brain in Mind* (2000) by Eric Jensen

*Tools for Engagement* (2003) by Eric Jensen

# About the Author

Eric Jensen is a visionary educator who is committed to making a positive, significant, and lasting difference in the way we learn. He's a member of the prestigious Society for Neuroscience and New York Academy of Sciences. A former middle-school teacher and college instructor, Jensen is the author of more than a dozen books on learning and teaching. He co-founded the world's first experimental brain-compatible academic enrichment program in 1982 that now has more than 30,000 graduates. Currently, he's a staff developer and consultant living in San Diego, California.

## Other Books by Eric Jensen

*SuperTeaching, Tools for Engagement, The Learning Brain, Brain-Based Learning, Trainer's Bonanza, Teaching with the Brain in Mind, Joyful Fluency* (with Lynn Dhority), *The Great Memory Book* (with Karen Markowitz), *Learning with the Body in Mind, Different Brains, Different Learners*, and *Learning Smarter*.

## Author Contact

Fax (858) 642-0404 or email at eric@jlcbrain.com

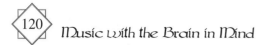

# Index

**CORWIN PRESS**

The Corwin Press logo—a raven striding across an open book—represents the union of courage and learning. Corwin Press is committed to improving education for all learners by publishing books and other professional development resources for those serving the field of PreK–12 education. By providing practical, hands-on materials, Corwin Press continues to carry out the promise of its motto: **"Helping Educators Do Their Work Better."**